HSE

Health and safety in roof work

HSE Books

First published 1987
Second edition 1998
Third edition 2008
Reprint with amends 2010
Fourth edition 2012
Reprinted 2012

ISBN 978 0 7176 6527 3

Acknowledgements

This guidance has been written with the help of the members of the Advisory Committee for Roofsafety (ACR) (www.roofworkadvice.info), including:

BCSA	British Constructional Steelwork Association Ltd (www.steelconstruction.org)
BSIF	British Safety Industry Federation, Height Safety Group (www.bsif.co.uk)
CTMA	Concrete Tile Manufacturers Association (www.britishprecast.org)
EPIC	Engineered Panels in Construction (www.epic.uk.com)
FASET	Fall Arrest Safety Equipment Training (www.faset.org.uk)
FCMA	Fibre Cement Manufacturers Association
FRA	Flat Roofing Alliance (www.nfrc.co.uk/FRA.aspx)
MCRMA	Metal Cladding and Roofing Manufacturers Association (www.mcrma.co.uk)
NARM	National Association of Rooflight Manufacturers (www.narm.org.uk)
NFRC	National Federation of Roofing Contractors Limited (www.nfrc.co.uk)
RIDBA	Rural and Industrial Design and Building Association (www.ridba.org.uk)
SPRA	Single Ply Roofing Association (www.spra.co.uk)
WAHSA	Work at Height Safety Association (www.wahsa.org.uk)

Contents

Preface

Every year many construction site workers are killed or injured because of their work, and many others suffer ill health. The hazards are not, however, restricted to those working on sites. Children and other members of the public are also killed or injured because construction activities have not been adequately controlled.

The construction industry's performance has steadily improved, but the rates of death, serious injury and ill health are still the highest of all industries. These deaths, injuries and ill health cause pain and suffering. They also have a cost in industrial injuries claims, medical treatment, and lost time at work.

The aim of this book is to help all those involved in construction – specifically roof work activities (including activities often not considered as roof work, such as maintenance and surveying) – to identify the main causes of accidents and ill health and to explain how to identify the hazards and prevent or control the risks. The guidance is simple and will have general relevance to everyone in the construction process, but particularly to those directly involved in roof work. It will refer to other documents, some relevant to particular groups, depending on the subject they address.

Introduction

Why is this guidance needed?

1 Working on roofs is a high-risk activity because it involves work at height. Roofers account for 24% of all workers who are killed in falls from height while at work. Falls through fragile materials, such as roof lights and asbestos cement roofing sheets, account for more of these deaths than any other single cause. There are also many serious injuries, often resulting in permanent disabilities.

2 Remember that not all those who are killed or injured while working on roofs are trained roofers – many people accessing roofs are in fact carrying out other tasks, ie maintenance and surveying.

3 These accidents occur across the whole range of roof work from the simplest repairs to large-scale construction projects (see Figures 1 and 2).

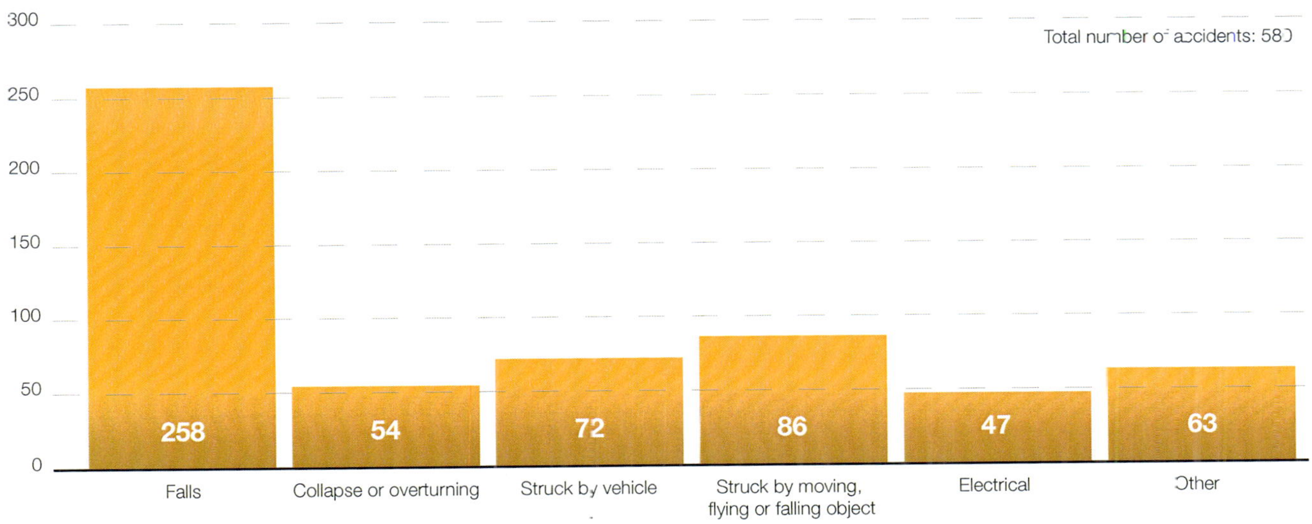

Figure 1 Falls are the biggest killer in construction (Fatal accidents in construction 1999 – January 2007)

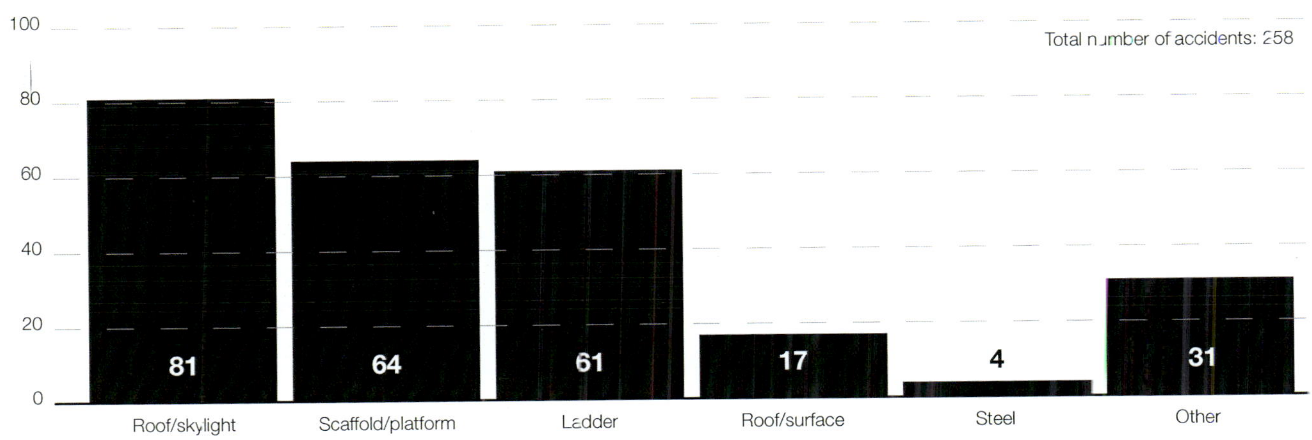

Figure 2 Most fatal falls are from roofs (Fatalities resulting from falls in construction 1999 – January 2007)

What is this book about?

4 This book contains guidance on how to plan and work safely on roofs. It covers new buildings, repair, maintenance, cleaning work and demolition. It also includes some guidance for those not directly carrying out the work on the roof, eg clients, designers and specifiers.

5 The main problems that need to be addressed are falls through fragile roofing materials and falls from unprotected roof edges. In most cases, straightforward physical protection measures can prevent accidents occurring but too often a lack of foresight and poor management control mean that protection is neglected during high-risk work, leading to accidents.

A roofer was part of a gang who were re-sheeting a large steel portal frame warehouse. Approximately 50% of the roof was netted underneath. The roofer was moving a sheet from a storage pile at the opposite end of the building when he fell through an uncovered fragile roof light in an area of the roof that was not protected by nets.

A 50-year-old maintenance worker was killed when he fell through a fragile roof light panel as he was checking roof repair work carried out by other contractors. The covers, which had been provided when the repair work was carried out, had been removed and the roof light panels were unprotected.

6 Not all the safeguards in this guidance will be relevant in all circumstances. Those who are planning the work should consider the extent and nature of the risks in the specific job and then plan a safe method of work from there. The guidance is structured to identify precautions that are applicable to all roof work. It also includes precautions that are particularly relevant to different types of roof and different types of work. However, risks are significant in all roof work and high standards of safety are necessary to provide adequate protection.

Who should read this book?

7 Roof work is not just an issue for construction companies. Other workers, such as building maintenance staff, can fall from or through roofs. This guidance will be useful to anyone planning, arranging or supervising roof work or work on roofs including:

- directors and partners of companies who carry out roof work;
- clients of projects involving roof work;
- designers and specifiers of buildings and components;
- CDM (Construction (Design and Management) Regulations 2007) co-ordinators;
- principal contractors for projects that include roof work;
- owners of buildings where roof work may take place;
- trade union safety representatives and employees' safety representatives;
- anyone carrying out roof work, including employees and the self-employed; and
- safety consultants and advisers.

Other useful information sources

8 This book does not repeat detailed guidance available about other topics or equipment common to construction work in general. However, the reference section gives a list of useful publications and indicates where you can find such advice.

The law

9 There is a range of law relevant to roof work safety. The principal elements are:

- the Health and Safety at Work etc Act 1974;
- the Work at Height Regulations 2005;
- the Management of Health and Safety at Work Regulations 1999;
- the Construction (Design and Management) Regulations 2007;
- the Lifting Operations and Lifting Equipment Regulations 1998; and
- the Provision and Use of Work Equipment Regulations 1998.

10 *Health and safety in construction* HSG150[1] contains more information on these legal requirements.

Planning for safety

11 Planning is vital to ensure safety in any size of building or roof work project, from short-duration minor work, such as replacing a few tiles on a house, to the major refurbishment of an existing property. Planning by all parties involved helps to make sure the work is carried out safely, efficiently and without undue delay.

12 Where they apply, the Construction (Design and Management) Regulations 2007 (CDM) identify the role of each party of a construction contract and set out specific guidelines for them to follow. For more information, see chapter 'Construction (Design and Management) Regulations 2007'.

13 However, not all roof work is carried out as part of a construction contract and in many cases, if it was, CDM would not apply, especially in respect of repairs and maintenance. It is therefore essential that the hazards associated with working at height are recognised and understood by the client or customer who commissions or arranges for the work to be carried out and the designer, where there is one. (Note that a designer may be a contractor who produces a specification or scheme of work and may not be a professional design or architectural practice.)

14 The client or customer must make sure that the individual or company they have employed to carry out roof work is competent to do so and is aware of the hazards and precautions to be taken for the work to be carried out safely. (For more information see paragraphs 18–26 and 300–315.) They should also make sure that any materials selected will not create additional hazards for future maintenance, access or demolition of the property (see paragraphs 317–325).

15 Because roof work usually involves work at height, it is important to prevent or minimise risk when planning this work; take a sensible risk-based approach to identify suitable precautions. As part of this planning process, you must consider the Work at Height Regulations 2005 as falls are the biggest cause of accidental death in the construction industry, accounting for 50% of all fatalities. In these Regulations there is no distinction between low and high falls, so for any work at height, no matter how high or low, precautions are required to prevent or minimise the risk of injury from a fall.

Hierarchy for work at height

16 The Work at Height Regulations 2005 set out a hierarchy of fall protection measures to be taken when planning work at height. The hierarchy has to be followed systematically and only when one level is not reasonably practicable may the next level down be considered.

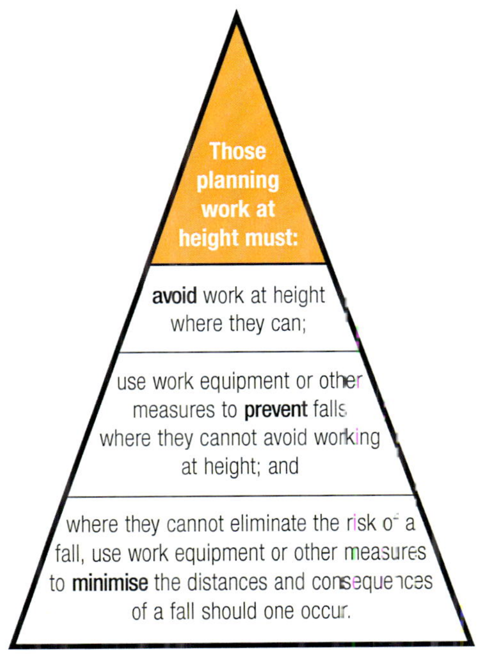

Figure 3 Hierarchy for work at height

17 Those in control of the work must also:

- always consider measures that protect everyone who is at risk (ie collective protection systems such as scaffolds, nets or soft landing systems) before measures that only protect the individual (ie personal protection measures such as a harnesses);
- always consider passive systems such as nets (where the individual does not have to do anything to activate the system) before active systems such as harnesses (where the worker has to clip on); and
- make sure work is carried out only when weather conditions do not put the health and safety of workers in danger.

See Table 1 and paragraph 45 for practical examples.

Training and competency

18 As stated in paragraph 1, roof work is a high-risk activity, so it is essential that anyone wishing to have roof work carried out makes sure that the contractors they choose to carry out the work are competent to do so.

19 A contractor should be able to demonstrate:

- sufficient knowledge of the particular type of roof work they are being asked to carry out and the risks it will entail; and
- current and sufficient experience of the latest techniques, standards and materials to enable them to carry the work out safely, including any relevant training or qualifications. This training should cover safe working practices and, if required, the selection, pre-use inspection and use of personal fall protection equipment.

20 It is important that contractors have up-to-date knowledge, experience and training, as although experience is a major factor, if it is based on poor or inadequate initial training or out-of-date knowledge it can be worthless. People must understand the reasons why safe working practices are necessary.

21 It is also helpful to ask whether the contractor has adequate resources to be able to complete the job safely, such as providing suitable on-site supervision and manpower.

22 Checking whether a contractor is a member of a reputable trade organisation is also useful as some provide guarantees, have a complaints procedure, and inspect the credentials of members and their work. Trade organisations such as the National Federation of Roofing Contractors, the Flat Roofing Alliance, the Single Ply Roofing Association, the Mastic Asphalt Council and the Rural and Industrial Design and Building Association offer such assurances.

23 For more information on competence and training see paragraphs 300–315. For work where CDM applies, a 'Core criteria for demonstration of competence' assessment has been produced in Appendix 4 of *Managing health and safety in construction. Construction (Design and Management) Regulations 2007. Approved Code of Practice* L144.[2]

Method statements

24 A competent person should prepare a safety method statement before work starts on a roof. It needs to be appropriate to the scale and complexity of the work. In all cases, it should make sure that risks are recognised and assessed, and the appropriate control measures specified. It should identify working positions, access routes to the roof and on the roof, and show:

- how falls are to be prevented, or where this is not possible, minimised;
- how danger to those at work below, and to the public, from falling materials is to be controlled;
- how risks to health will be controlled;
- how other risks identified at planning and survey stages are to be controlled, eg handling hot bitumen;
- what equipment will be needed;
- what competence and/or training is needed;
- who will supervise the job 'on site';
- how changes in the work will be dealt with without affecting safe working; and
- who will check that the system is effectively controlling risk.

25 Safety method statements should be clear and illustrated by simple sketches where necessary. There should be no ambiguities or generalisations, which could lead to confusion. They should be produced for the benefit of those carrying out the work and their immediate supervisors and not be over complicated.

26 Equipment needed for safe working should be clearly identified and available before work starts. Workers should know what to do if the work method needs to be changed. This should then avoid 'ad hoc' methods of work on site and the use of improvised equipment, which can often lead to accidents. See Appendix 1 for further information.

Fragility

27 Falling through a fragile roof is one of the main causes of accidents during roof work, occurring in both the construction of new roofs and maintenance of old ones, so it is important to consider fragility when planning any roof work task. Despite the fact that the installation of 'non-fragile' roofs, including roof lights, in new buildings is now commonplace, people who work on roofs should not be complacent, as eventually even these materials will become fragile due to a number of factors:

- the fixings were badly secured, leading to excessive wear around the fixing;
- the fixing washers have failed due to over-tightening, leading to sheet and fixing corrosion;
- the protective surface of the profiled sheeting was damaged by foot traffic during construction or during the roof maintenance phase, which will lead to an early breakdown of the sheet's performance;
- any slip or fall on to the roof may damage the assembly, which could lead to early corrosion failure;
- external atmospheric conditions (eg saline or factory processes) may lead to early failure of the sheet's performance; or
- the sheets and fixings have reached the end of their design performance.

28 All roofs should be treated as fragile until a competent person has confirmed they are not (see Appendix 4).

Safe access to the roof

29 Safe access to a work area requires careful planning, particularly where work progresses along the roof. Typical methods to access roofs are:

- general access scaffolds;
- stair towers;
- fixed or mobile scaffold towers;
- mobile access equipment;
- ladders; and
- roof access hatches.

More detailed advice on the selection and use of access equipment is given in *Health and safety in construction* HSG150.

General access scaffolds

30 A general access scaffold can provide safe access to roof level and a working platform around the edge of the roof, as well as providing space to store materials. Often, a loading bay can be erected and can help materials handling on the roof.

31 You should follow this good practice when using scaffolds:

- scaffolds should be designed, erected, altered and dismantled only by competent people and the work should be carried out under the direction of a competent supervisor;
- scaffolds should never be erected or dismantled over people or busy pavements. If the work presents a danger to the public you should apply for a road or pavement closure to eliminate the risk of a member of the public being injured. If this is not granted, erection and dismantling should be done inside a segregated area and during times when there are fewer members of the public in the vicinity;
- scaffolds should be based on a firm, level foundation. The ground or foundation should be capable of supporting the weight of the scaffold and any loads likely to be placed upon it. Be aware of any voids, such as basements or drains, and patches of soft, uneven ground, which could collapse when loaded. Provide extra support as necessary; and
- scaffold should be braced and tied to a permanent structure or otherwise stabilised. Proprietary system scaffolds should be erected and tied in accordance with the manufacturer's instructions, which should be available from the retailer when the scaffold is hired or purchased.

32 On sites where people from more than one trade are working, the principal contractor and the roofing contractor should agree what is necessary and who will provide it. They should also agree who will carry out the necessary statutory inspections. Make sure that scaffolds are suitable and safe before your employees use them.

Tower scaffolds and stair towers

33 Tower scaffolds and stair towers can provide safe access if they are erected by a competent person and used correctly. However, inappropriate erection and misuse of tower scaffolds cause a number of accidents each year. Aluminium towers are light and can easily overturn if used incorrectly. Towers rely on all parts being in place to ensure adequate strength – they can collapse if sections are left out.

34 The manufacturer or supplier has a duty to provide an instruction manual that explains the erection sequence, including any bracing requirements, and the height to which the tower can be erected safely. If the tower has been hired, the hirer has a duty to provide this information to their customer, who in turn must pass the information on to the workers erecting the tower.

35 Workers who erect towers should be trained and competent people who are following a safe method of work. There are two approved methods recommended by the Prefabricated Access Suppliers' and Manufacturers' Association (PASMA), which have been developed in co-operation with the Health and Safety Executive (HSE): the 'advanced guard rail' system and 'through the trap' ('3T'). Advice on these two methods is given in *Health and safety in construction* HSG150 and *Tower scaffolds* CIS10.[3]

36 Stair tower designs are preferable to ladders as they allow materials such as small components or tools to be safely carried onto the roof.

A roofer, aged 24, was killed when he fell from the edge of an industrial roof. He was doing re-sheeting work and a tower scaffold was provided for access to the roof level. Even with the outriggers in use, the tower was inadequately tied and so was unstable. The guard rails were also poorly fitted.

Figure 4 Stair towers provide good access. Make sure they are properly secured and erected (Image courtesy of Turner Access)

Mobile access equipment

37 A wide range of mobile access equipment is available, most of which comes under the umbrella term of 'MEWP' (mobile elevating work platform). There are three basic types:

- scissor lift (which gives a vertical lift only);
- telescopic boom (which gives vertical lift and outreach and is generally known as a 'cherry picker'); and
- articulating and telescopic boom (which are often vehicle mounted).

38 For short-duration work, such as inspection and minor maintenance, MEWPs can provide excellent safe access to the roof. Risks associated with scaffold erection can often be avoided if mobile access equipment is used rather than scaffolding. However, the equipment chosen should be appropriate for the ground conditions on the site. Follow the manufacturer's advice on the maximum wind speed at which the MEWP can be safely operated.

39 Equipment should be maintained in a safe condition and be operated only by trained and competent workers. See *The selection and management of mobile elevating work platforms* CIS58.[4]

40 Where a MEWP is used as a means of access to the roof, the equipment should be designed to allow safe access from the MEWP to the roof.

Ladders

41 A third of all reported fall-from-height incidents involve ladders and stepladders; on average this accounts for 14 deaths and 1200 major injuries to workers each year. This is because, while ladders may provide safe access in some circumstances and despite being one of the most commonly used pieces of access equipment in the construction industry, they are often misused or inappropriate for the task.

42 Ask yourself:

- Is a ladder the best piece of access equipment to use in the first place?
- Is there a safer means that is further up the work at height hierarchy?
- What is the activity you are carrying out and how long might someone be working on the ladder?
- What length of ladder is required? Very long ladders are heavy to handle and may need staying to reduce flexing in use.
- Are workers expected to carry materials and tools or work on the ladder?
- Can the person using the ladder maintain three points of contact while on the ladder?

43 Where ladders are used, they need to be of the right type, ie a suitable grade of industrial ladder. They should be in good condition and effectively secured to prevent movement. They should also extend over the working platform level by at least 1 m to provide a safe handhold at the stepping off area. Inspect ladders regularly to make sure they have no visible defects, and where defects are found, take the ladder out of use until repaired.

A 48-year-old roofer was killed when he fell from an untied ladder as he attempted to carry bundles of tiles up it. The ladder was too short for the work in question and was being moved progressively along a wall while the work took place.

44 For more information and guidance on ladder use refer to:

- *Safe use of ladders and stepladders: An employers' guide* INDG402;[5]
- *A toolbox talk on leaning ladder and stepladder safety* INDG403;[6] and
- *Top tips for ladder and stepladder safety* INDG405.[7]

Safe place of work on the roof

45 A safe place of work, including safe access, should be provided for all roof work. There is a clear hierarchy for all work at height (see Figure 3); it helps guide those people planning the work to provide the safest possible work area.

Table 1 Practical examples of solutions using the hierarchy for work at height

The hierarchy	Example solutions
Avoid the need to work at height	Use a telescopic pole with a camera attachment to conduct roof inspections.
Where work at height cannot be avoided:	
Prevent a fall	A non-fragile roof with a 1 m high parapet all the way round provides an existing safe place of work.
	Use edge protection (boarded scaffold with guard rails/netting) and suitable safe access onto the roof, eg a stair tower.
	Mobile elevating work platforms (MEWPs) can provide a safe working platform to work from.
	Use a work-restraint system (eg harness with a short lanyard, which means it is impossible for the operative to get to a position where they could fall).
Where the risk of a fall cannot be prevented:	
Minimise the consequences of a fall, should one occur	Use safety nets to protect everyone working in the area. Use beanbags or inflatable air-bag systems, rigged close under the work surface.
	Personal fall-arrest systems are the last resort as they do not prevent the fall, only mitigate the consequences, and only protect the individual worker.
	Training, instruction and other means, such as providing adequate lighting, personal protective equipment (PPE) and supervision, can also mitigate the consequences of a fall.

Emergency rescue procedures

46 Under the Work at Height Regulations 2005, emergency procedures must be considered for circumstances such as stuck access equipment and deployed fall arrest, so that a person or people can be rescued. There must be a plan in place that outlines how someone would be recovered should they fall.

47 The method of rescue needs to be proportionate to the risk and you should not rely on the emergency services. The method of rescue may be simple, such as putting a ladder up to a net and allowing the fallen person to descend, or lowering a worker hanging on a deployed lanyard onto the surface below. Once the rescue has been completed, standard first-aid procedures are recommended including use of the standard horizontal recovery position where necessary: www.hse.gov.uk/firstaid/index.htm.

48 A casualty who is experiencing symptoms such as light-headedness, nausea, sensations of flushing, tingling or numbness of the arms or legs, anxiety, visual disturbance or faintness, or who is unconscious while suspended in a harness should be rescued as soon as is safely possible. Elevation of the legs by the casualty or rescuer (where safely possible) may enable them to tolerate suspension for longer.

49 An emergency 999 ambulance or equivalent qualified paramedical or medical provider should be called for anyone who becomes unconscious in harness or rope suspension, whether apparently recovered or not. Removal to hospital is deemed unnecessary if there is no loss of consciousness and no apparent or suspected injury and the subject is without other symptoms, ie they have had a short fall for a short period of time in suspension and either self rescued or been lowered from suspension.

50 In some situations, you may need to consider using other work equipment, such as MEWPs, man-riding baskets for cranes or proprietary rescue systems. Whatever system or method you decide on, include this information in the construction phase plan (where CDM applies) or in the method statement for the work. You should use the method statement to brief people who will be working at height and involved in a rescue plan.

51 The rescue plan should include:

- details of the rescue equipment to be used;
- configuration of the equipment for different types of rescue;
- identification of anchor points where necessary;
- limitations of the plan for adverse weather such as high winds; and
- the need for trained rescue personnel.

Materials handling

A roofer working with his teenage son died when he fell from a tied access ladder. He was carrying rolls of roofing membrane up the ladder when one caught on the eaves and caused him to lose his balance and fall.

52 Well-planned materials handling has a significant impact on roof work safety, eg it can:

- minimise the amount of time spent working at height;
- reduce the amount of travelling around the roof to collect materials;
- reduce injuries caused by handling heavy and unwieldy components, eg large roof sheets or roof trusses;
- increase productivity; and
- reduce waste.

53 On smaller roofing jobs, small lifting appliances (such as a gin wheel, gantry hoist or scaffold hoist) may be used. They are usually mounted near the edge of a roof so it is important that suitable guard rails and toe boards are installed to prevent the workers using the appliance from falling. See Figure 5(b).

54 Lifting appliances of this type need a secure anchorage. When counterweights are used they must allow a safety factor of not less than three. If a gin wheel is used, you should allow for the force exerted by the person who is raising the load (see Figures 6(a) and (b)).

55 Secure counterweights to the tail of the appliance to prevent removal or interference. Avoid using rolls of felt, blocks of bitumen etc, as they are liable to be removed and used in the roofing operation.

56 Where practicable, guard rails and toe boards should remain in position when material is being raised or lowered. If (unusually) they have to be removed, anyone who needs to be near the edge, eg for signalling or to help move the load, should wear a safety harness in work restraint mode and attached to a suitable anchorage point (see Appendix 3). The harness should only allow them to reach the edge to pull the materials in, no further, so they are never in a position from which they could fall.

57 All hooks used in lifting operations should be fitted with safety catches.

58 Every lifting appliance should be properly installed, maintained, inspected and, at all times, operated within its safe working load. All lifting appliances need a periodic thorough inspection. Please refer to *Lifting equipment at work: A brief guide to the law* INDG290 (see Further reading).

59 Access to the area below a lifting point should be strictly controlled, eg by temporary 1 m high fencing which is secured and well signed.

Falling materials

60 The public, as well as other workers, can be at risk when materials fall from roofs. These materials include roof sheets, fixings, tools, roof tiles, membranes, roofing (felt) and hot bitumen. At the planning stage of any job, consider what measures are needed to protect the public and other workers. More information is given in paragraphs 228–236 – many of the measures described here will also be required to protect people at work. There are many measures you can use, such as debris nets, properly designed scaffold fans and covered walkways.

Figure 5(a) Industrial hoist (Images courtesy of HSS)

Figure 5(b) Domestic hoist

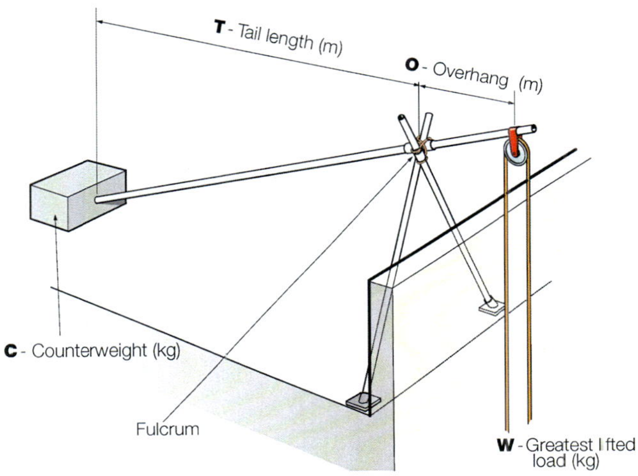

Figure 6(a) Counterweight anchorage for a gin wheel

61 The safest option for removing waste materials from a roof is to use a rubble chute. See Figure 7.

A member of the public was seriously injured when hit by tiles thrown from a roof while it was being stripped. The use of a waste chute would have prevented the accident (see Figure 7).

Notes to Figure 6(a):

- Total anticipated load, allowing for the pull on the opposite side of the wheel from the load to be lifted is 2.5 x **W**.
- Allowing for a safety factor of 3, **C** x **T** must not be less than 3 x (2.5 x **W** x **O**).

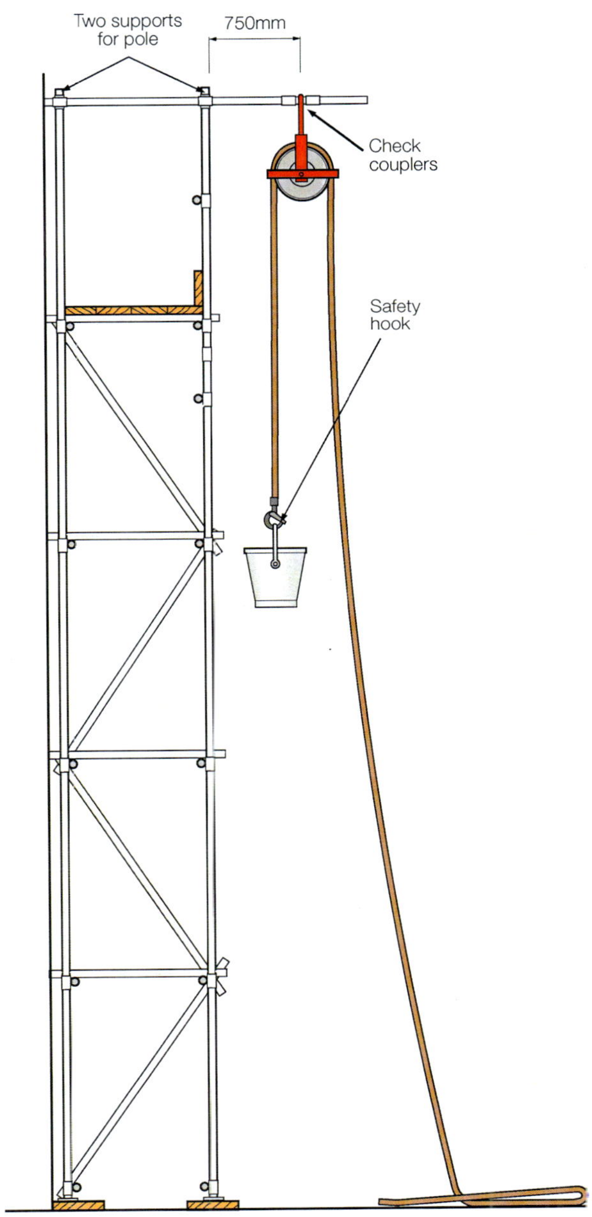

Figure 6(b) Properly erected gin wheel (ties not shown)

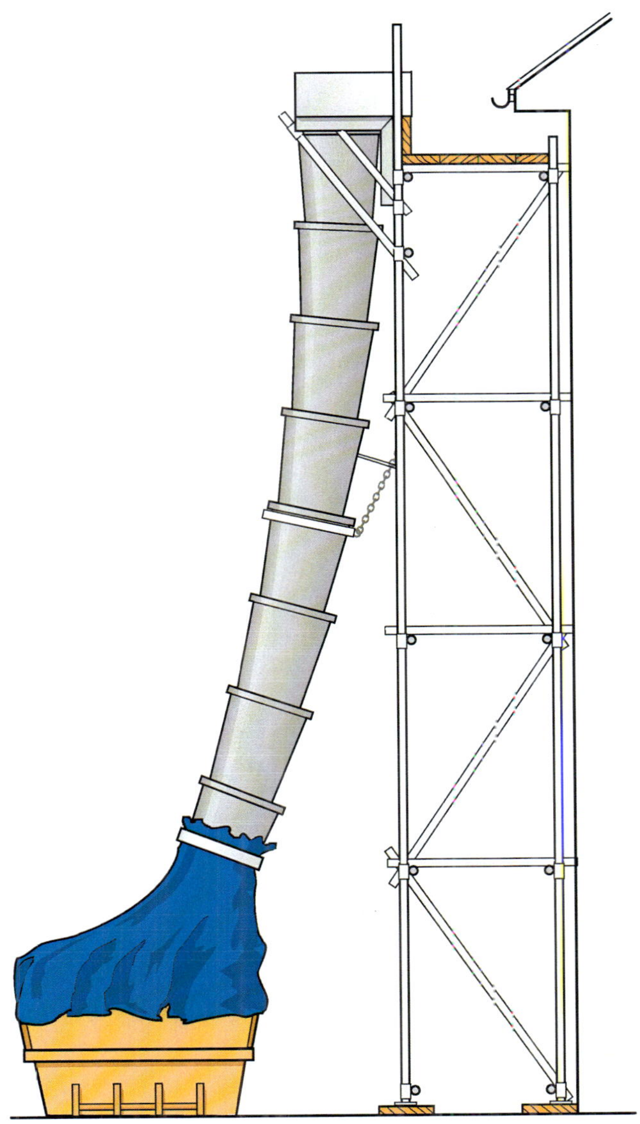

Figure 7 Waste chutes make waste handling easier and safer

62 Control access by other trades when roof workers are working overhead as there is risk of falling materials. You should consider this when programming overlapping work. Where work is carried out below roof workers, effective measures will be required to prevent injury, such as birdcage scaffold or suitable debris netting (see Figure 8).

Figure 8 Debris netting used in addition to safety netting may enable work to be carried out safely below roof workers

A client (a major supermarket chain) identified and provided additional resources for the installation of safety nets and debris netting during the roofing phase of a new 'superstore'. This allowed the roof workers to work quickly and safely within the protection of the nets. The addition of debris netting also allowed work to be carried out below them as the risk from falling materials was controlled. As a result, delays were minimised and savings were made on labour costs.

Weather conditions

63 You should anticipate adverse weather conditions and take suitable precautions. The Work at Height Regulations 2005 specifically require that weather conditions be considered when planning any work at height. Rain, ice or snow can turn a secure footing into a skating rink. A roof should always be inspected before work starts to see if conditions have changed and to check whether it is safe to work.

64 A sudden gust of wind can lead to loss of balance. Roof sheets and, in some circumstances, roofing membrane should not be fixed in windy weather as people can easily be thrown off-balance while carrying a sheet up to or on the roof, particularly when handling large sheeting materials during work on industrial buildings.

65 It is not only in industrial roofing that care must be taken in windy conditions. A slater or tiler cannot work safely in high winds and a roll of roofing membrane can become mobile if it is caught by the wind. On flat roofs, materials such as felts are equally affected and the effect of high wind upon hot bitumen when it is being poured can be extremely dangerous.

66 When deciding whether to continue or suspend work, consider:

- wind speed;
- the measures that have already been taken to prevent falls from the roof; and
- the position and height of the roof and the size of the material being handled.

67 A competent contractor should use a hand-held anemometer to measure wind speed if large sheets are being handled.

68 The Beaufort scale (Table 2) gives descriptions of how trees, smoke etc will behave at certain wind speeds.

Table 2 The Beaufort scale

No	m/s	mph	Description	Effects on land
0	0	0	Calm	Smoke rises vertically
3	4	8–12	Gentle breeze	Gentle breeze, small twigs in constant motion
4	6	13–18	Moderate wind	Dust, leaves and loose paper raised. Small branches move
5	8	19–24	Fresh wind	Fresh breeze. Small trees in leaf begin to sway
6	10	25–31	Strong wind	Strong breeze, large branches move. Whistling heard in phone wires. Umbrellas become difficult to use
7	14–16	32–38	Very strong wind	Whole trees in motion
8	18–20	39–46	Gale	Twigs break off trees. Difficult to walk
9	22–24	47–54	Severe gale	Slight structural damage occurs – chimney pots and slates removed
10	26	55–63	Storm	Trees uprooted. Structural damage

69 Sites should be inspected at the end of the working day to make sure that loose materials, especially sheets, offcuts and fixings, are not left unsecured on the roof.

70 Tables 3–8 have been reproduced by kind permission of the National Federation of Roofing Contractors (NFRC) from its guide to work in windy conditions.[8]

Roofing work

Table 3 Maximum wind speed for sheeting and decking

Roofing activity	Wind speed at which activity should cease
All laying or handling of profiled single-skin sheets at roof level	Mean (average) wind speed reaches 23 mph (gusting to 35 mph or over)
All laying or handling of sheets longer than 5 m at roof level	Mean wind speed reaches 17 mph (gusting to 26 mph or over)
Where multi-skin construction is in progress, eg laying or handling lightweight materials (such as glass fibre, insulation boards, liner trays etc) at roof level	Mean wind speed reaches 17 mph (gusting to 26 mph or over)

71 Special consideration must be given to laying and handling sheets exceeding 20 m in length. The above maximum wind speeds may be too high, as the surface area of the sheet may make it unwieldy in lower wind speeds.

Table 4 Maximum wind speed for slating and tiling

Activity	Wind speed at which activity should cease
All laying or handling of slates, tiles, battens and felt at roof level	Mean wind speed reaches 23 mph (gusting to 35 mph or over)
Handling rolls of felt at roof level – extreme care should be taken	Mean wind speeds are in the region of 17 mph (gusting to 26 mph or over)

72 As long as this work is carried out from a safe working platform or safe scaffolding, it should be possible to provide additional protection at the work position, which should render the limitations of working in windy conditions less significant than when working directly on a roof. However, every situation should be considered individually as local conditions may increase the hazards.

Table 5 Maximum wind speed for reinforced bitumen membrane roofing

Activity	Wind speed at which activity should cease
All laying or handling of felt and hot bitumen at roof level	Mean wind speed reaches 23 mph (gusting to 35 mph or over)
Handling rolls of lightweight felt and/or working with 'hot bitumen' – extreme care is necessary	Mean wind speeds in the region of 17 mph (gusting to 26 mph or over)

Table 6 Maximum wind speed for work with mastic asphalt

Activity	Wind speed at which activity should cease
All laying or handling of mastic asphalt at roof level	Mean wind speed reaches 23 mph (gusting to 35 mph or over)
All laying or handling of felt, insulation boards or hot bitumen at roof level	Mean wind speed reaches 23 mph (gusting to 35 mph or over)
Handling rolls of lightweight felt and/or working with hot bitumen – extreme care is necessary	Mean wind speeds in the region of 17 mph (gusting to 26 mph or over)

Table 7 Maximum wind speed for work with membrane roof coverings

Activity	Wind speed at which activity should cease
All laying or handling of membrane roof coverings at roof level	Mean wind speed reaches 23 mph (gusting to 35 mph or over)

73 The practical application of a membrane system will, however, cause work to be stopped at wind speeds lower than the 23 mph limit.

Vertical work

Table 8 Guide to maximum wind speed for cladding

Activity	Wind speed at which activity should cease
All fixing or handling of sheets more than 2 m above ground level	Mean wind speed reaches 23 mph (gusting to 35 mph or over)
All fixing or handling of sheets longer than 5 m when more than 2 m above ground level	Mean wind speed reaches 17 mph (gusting to 26 mph or over)
Where multi-layer construction is in progress, all fixing or handling of lightweight materials (such as glass fibre, insulation boards, liner trays etc) more than 2 m above ground level	Mean wind speed reaches 17 mph (gusting to 26 mph or over)

74 Special consideration must be given when fixing or handling cladding sheets that are of exceptional length. The above maximum speeds may be too high, as the surface area of the sheet may make it unwieldy in lower wind speeds.

Electricity at work

75 Contact with overhead electric power lines is a regular cause of death and injury. Any work near overhead electric power lines or railway power lines must be carefully planned to avoid accidental contact. This is particularly relevant where long conducting objects such as scaffold tubes, metal roof sheets or ladders are likely to be manoeuvred near to power lines. Generally, working underneath or near to overhead electric power lines should be avoided.

76 Designers should consider changing the footprint of the building or discuss relocating lines with the owner to eliminate the risk of contact during construction and maintenance. Where roof workers have to work near overhead lines, designers should also review the length of metal roof sheets and any other long conducting objects such as metal finishing strips.

77 Principal contractors should discuss the necessary precautions with the owners to avoid accidental contact of the overhead power line. Such precautions may require power lines to be switched off and made safe to eliminate the risk of contact. In some cases it may be possible for the owner of the power line to sheath the conductors. You will need to pre-plan the work to enable the line owner to make provision for such arrangements.

Two workers were electrocuted while carrying out external maintenance works to soffits and bargeboards. The rear of the property was inaccessible so they tried to gain access from an adjacent field. While attempting to place a two-stage aluminium ladder over the boundary the ladder came into contact with an 11 kV overhead line.

A roof worker was electrocuted when moving an aluminium ladder that contacted an 11 kV power line. He was repairing storm damage to the roof. The power lines ran parallel to the eaves less than 2 m away.

78 Clients and owners should make roofers aware of where existing electricity supplies run on their property before any roof work starts. This will ensure that the work to be carried out will not bring them into contact with the supply, or if it is likely to, measures can be put in place to make electricity conductors dead or, in some cases, sheath them for the duration of the job.

79 It is also important to remember that use of portable electrical tools can create hazards. For example, metal roof sheet edges can damage cable insulation. All electrical supplies to portable tools should be obtained from properly constructed and installed plugs and sockets of the industrial type. Where possible, battery-operated tools should be used. If this is not practicable, a reduced low-voltage system (sometimes referred to as 110-volt centre tapped to earth (CTE) system) should be used. All electrical equipment should be properly installed and maintained (see BS 7375:2010[9]).

80 The electricity companies (distribution network operators (DNOs)) that own the majority of overhead power lines are concerned about the lack of pre-planned contact they received from construction companies. Often, requests are received for advice when the job is in progress and the DNO is accused of being unhelpful because they will not switch off lines or re-route at short notice. There are often very good reasons why this cannot be done. Companies should work closely with the DNO to agree precautions **before** work begins.

Escape in case of fire

81 You should consider how to escape from the roof in case of fire. A fire could result from:

- construction work on a roof, eg welding or hot work using bitumen; or
- activities inside a building, including those under refurbishment.

82 In either case, the means of escape from the roof must be adequate, agreed and communicated before work begins. How complex this needs to be depends on the risk of being trapped if there is a fire. It could mean, for example, making sure that mobile access equipment is always available in case of an emergency, or providing additional stair towers or (tied) ladders.

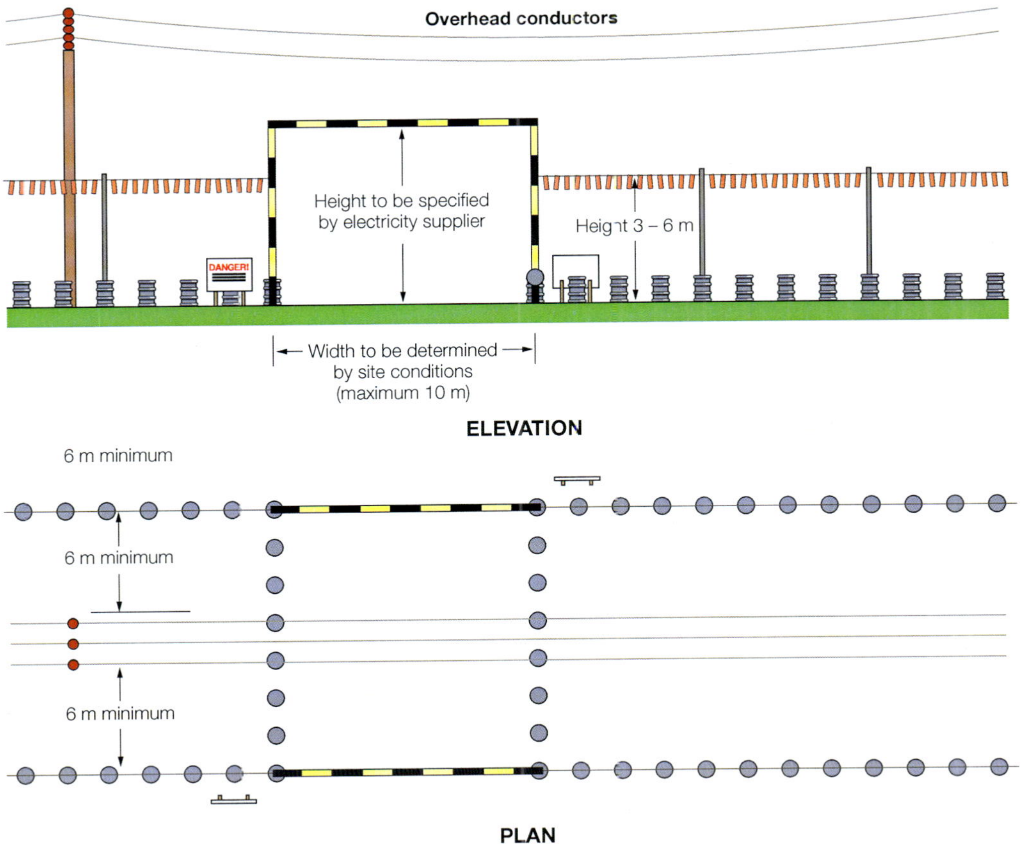

Figure 9 Diagram showing normal dimension for 'goal post' crossing points and barriers where plant is operating. Similar markings could be used to mark overhead power lines if long roof sheets or scaffold poles are being used

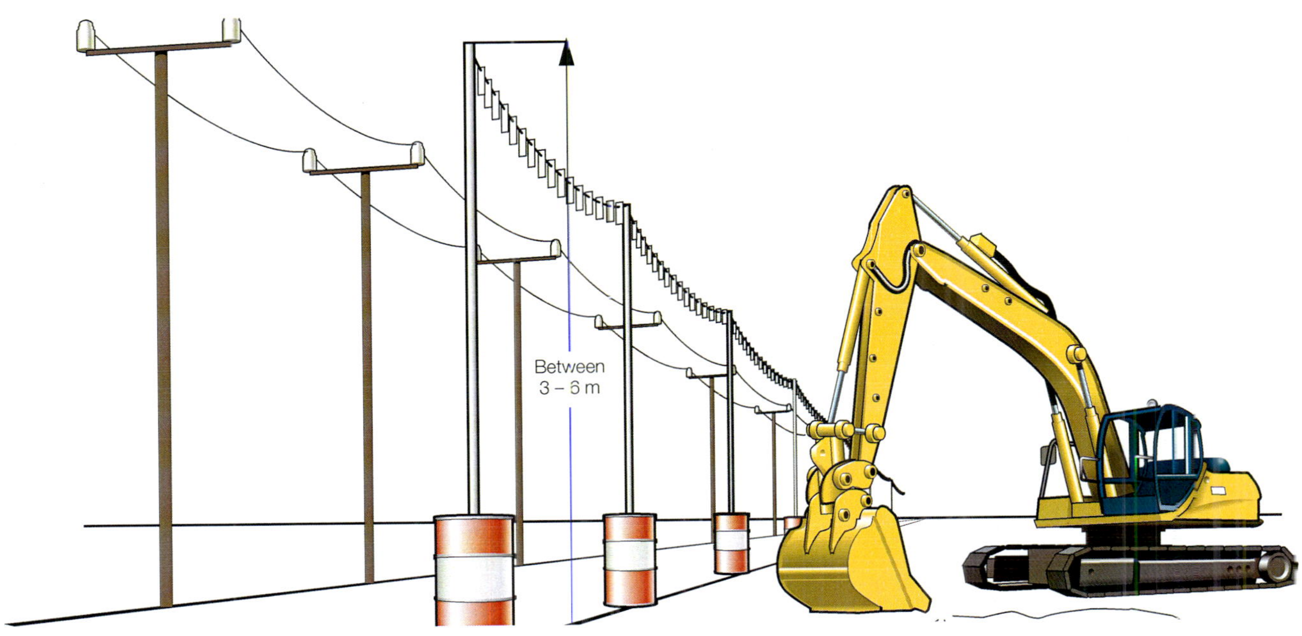

Figure 10 Ground-level barrier where plant is in use. A similar system could be used to mark overhead power lines if scaffold poles or long roof sheets are being used

Types of work

83 There are many reasons why someone may need to work on a roof, ranging from minor inspection to major re-roofing works. There are also many other reasons for accessing roofs, such as servicing or maintaining plant, installing or adjusting aerials or cleaning gutters. As a result, there are various safeguards to consider, depending on the type of work planned.

Inspection

84 Inspection is often necessary where a problem has been identified (eg a leak) or before refurbishment. It should always be done with care and by people trained and experienced in assessing the risks involved. Initially, in accordance with the hierarchy, work at height should be avoided where possible – eg by remote inspection using mast photography or videography where only visual inspection is required. The operator remains at ground level and controls the direction and zoom of the camera that is elevated on a mast. The pictures are then fed live to a screen where they can be viewed immediately. When using such systems, operators should take care to avoid overhead hazards such as electrical cables. See Figure 11.

85 Where you cannot avoid work at height, access to the roof should be planned and any risks associated with the work should be risk assessed and mitigated. If possible, the work should be carried out from a safe place. This could be from an adjacent structure, using binoculars or from mobile access equipment (see Figure 12) or a secured tower scaffold or ladder. Some investigations can be carried out from below if the roof structure is exposed.

86 If inspectors cannot avoid going onto a roof, they will be exposed to high risks, so high safety standards will be required.

87 Many modern roofs have fall-protection systems installed to allow gutter cleaning, maintenance and inspection. If they have been maintained and inspected properly by the client they should be used by those accessing the roof. However, people should be trained and competent to use the system before they are allowed on the roof.

Figure 11 Remote inspection mast with hand-held lightweight CCTV system (Image courtesy of Survey Support Ltd)

A self-employed surveyor fell from a surveyor's sectional ladder as he was measuring a dormer window at roof level. It is thought that he overreached and the top section of the ladder (which had not been fixed at the bottom) moved, causing him to fall with the ladder from the roof.

A managing director, aged 54, was killed when he fell through a fragile roof light panel as he was inspecting some repair work that had been completed on his premises roof.

88 Remember that all roof work is potentially dangerous, however short-lived.

Refurbishment and re-roofing

89 Roof refurbishment can be complex, is always high risk and demands careful planning – a high proportion of accidents occur where this work is being carried out.

- On any refurbishment or re-roofing job, all surfaces should be treated as fragile unless a competent person has confirmed otherwise (see Appendix 4).
- The precautions to prevent people falling through fragile parts of the roof should be clearly identified. They do not have to be complex but must be effective. The Work at Height Regulations 2005 require that no person at work should pass across or near or work on, from or near a fragile surface where it is reasonably practicable to carry out the work safely without them doing so.

90 To prevent accidents occurring:

- close liaison with the client will be necessary where premises remain occupied during refurbishment;
- a structural survey may be required to confirm the strength or stability of roof members; and
- a risk assessment should be carried out when deciding whether to refurbish or replace fragile roof coverings For example, the decision on whether to clean and seal or replace an existing asbestos fibre cement roof should take into account the additional risks from work at height, exposure to asbestos fibres and cost of future maintenance (see paragraph 256). Where cleaning is being planned, consider whether it is necessary – is it only being carried out for aesthetic reasons? If it is required, you must use a safe system (see paragraphs 183–198).

Ancillary works

91 There are many ancillary tasks carried out on roofs other than roof work, in particular, fitting or adjusting television aerials or solar panels to buildings. Anyone carrying out these tasks should have received relevant training for working at height on roofs to ensure their safety.

92 The Confederation of Aerial Industries Ltd has produced health and safety guidance and a code of practice for installation in the aerial and satellite industries.[10]

Maintenance and cleaning

93 Many accidents occur during maintenance and cleaning of roofs. Often little attention is paid to this short-term, low-value work. It is often done by people with no experience in work at height and often takes place on older roofs where extra care must be taken.

A casual worker, aged 23, was killed when he fell through a fragile roof light on an asbestos roof. He was power washing the roof of a farm building and stepped off one of the boards he was using as a work area on to the fragile roof light.

94 A high proportion of deaths are caused by falls through fragile materials, as in the example above. Any work on fragile roofs, however trivial it may seem, should be carefully assessed, planned and supervised.

95 People on roofs should also be competent to carry out the work. If introducing inexperienced workers, give them formal training on health and safety (specifically including the hazards associated with roofing, eg fragile materials, weather conditions, roof lights, and personal protective equipment they are required to use) before they go onto a roof and make sure they always work in an area where the supervisor can see them and speak to them.

96 Never allow inexperienced people to work on roofs unsupervised (see paragraphs 300–315 for more information).

97 Factors to take into account when assessing the risk include:

- roof lights, which may have been obscured by paint, debris or vegetation;
- any repairs carried out in the past, especially if fragile roof sheets have been used for 'patching' an otherwise non-fragile roof. Such practices are highly dangerous
- metal roof sheets, which may have deteriorated with age and become fragile;
- wood wool slabs, which may have been weakened by water damage; and
- safety systems that have been installed have been inspected and are ready for use.

For more information on fragile roofs see paragraphs 166–198.

98 A full survey, together with local knowledge, will help to identify such problems. In case of doubt, the roof should be treated as fragile. The precautions described for working on or near fragile materials should be rigorously followed whatever the size of the job.

Figure 12 Powered access for inspecting a large fragile roof

Figure 13 Valley walker used during gutter cleaning. This provides a protective mesh covering to either side of the operative, which moves progressively along the roof as the worker moves forward. The protective covering eliminates the risk of a fall through the fragile material (Image courtesy of Safesite Limited)

Roof cleaning

99 A typical example of cleaning on a roof is cleaning valley gutters on an asbestos cement roof or a roof containing fragile roof lights.

100 There are systems available that provide long-term protection for these regular operations, and you should consider them for existing roofs (see Figure 32). The alternative is to provide extensive temporary protection for each operation. This can be less cost-effective and requires rigorous supervision. Figures 13 and 14 show safe ways to both inspect and carry out some cleaning activities on fragile roofs.

A foreman was cleaning cement dust, which had spilled from a silo vent, when he fell 3.5 m through an asbestos cement roof. He was walking down the valley gutter, which was 300 mm wide. No protection had been provided for fragile material and no other precautions were taken to prevent falls. He died from head injuries.

Figure 14 Access system for short-term maintenance work on a fragile roof

Stripping and dismantling roofs

101 Stripping roofs to reclaim various roofing materials during demolition has often involved unsafe practices. An independent scaffold should be provided at eaves level to all elevations; this gives safe access to the roof and room for storage of materials. Inform the scaffolding contractor of the intended loading and take care not to exceed this. You may need to give specific guidance to site supervisors on the maximum number of tiles or slates per scaffold bay.

102 Timber battens deteriorate with age. Do not use them as footholds unless they have been inspected by a competent person who has confirmed that they are strong enough. If in doubt, regard them as fragile.

103 Never use timber battens as anchorage points for harnesses.

104 As the roof is stripped, you must take steps to prevent internal falls, for example, through the roof joists. There are various options available including:

- boarding out the roof joists to provide a suitable working platform;
- erecting a birdcage scaffold underneath the work area;
- crate or decking systems, which create a working floor underneath the work area (see Figure 15(a));
- bean/air bags as soft landing systems (see Figures 15(b) and 15(c));
- netting the underside of the roof;
- where ground conditions are stable, mobile access equipment could be considered;

- harnesses should be the last option considered, and only used where appropriate safe anchorage points are available and there is sufficient space clear of obstructions below the working position, should a fall occur.

Figure 15(a) Decking system that provides a working platform in the roof eaves (Image courtesy of Oxford Safety Components Ltd)

A teenager fell 10 m to his death while removing slates from a roof. The slates were being reclaimed before demolition. They were stored on a small area of flat roof adjacent to the pitched roof. He was loading the slates onto an inclined hoist when he fell. No edge protection was provided at the flat roof.

105 Mechanical handling devices and waste chutes (see Figures 5 and 7) are particularly useful in demolition where large quantities of waste and reclaimed materials are removed from roofs.

106 Demolition of buildings with fragile roof sheets or liners requires careful planning. CDM 2007 requires that all those (including clients) who appoint contractors are satisfied that they have the necessary competence and resources. **Resources include the time needed to plan and carry out the work safely.**

107 Asbestos cement sheet is a fragile material and cannot be relied upon to support someone's weight. If the asbestos cement sheets are in good condition and it is possible to provide safe access, preferably from underneath (eg using scissors lifts), then the sheets should be taken down whole from underneath. The sheets should not be dropped or damaged; they should be lowered to the floor and are best disposed of by careful transfer to covered vehicles or skips, or by wrapping intact in heavy-duty sheet plastic. For advice on disposal of waste asbestos sheets visit the Environment Agency website.[11]

Figure 15(b) Air bags being used as a fall mitigation measure during roof work (Image courtesy of Airtek Safety Products Ltd)

Figure 15(c) Bean bags being used as a fall mitigation measure during roofwork (Image courtesy of Forest Safety Products Ltd)

108 If the roofing sheets are in poor condition (ie liable to break when handled), or if safe access cannot be provided and the risk of falling is too great, then remote demolition is preferred. This could be by machine, such as a pusher arm or deliberate controlled collapse. In this case, you should follow the precautions outlined in Appendix 5 to control the spread of asbestos.

109 While remote demolition can be necessary in some cases, it should not be carried out without careful consideration. Where asbestos materials are involved, careful planning and suitable precautions to reduce the spread of asbestos fibres will be required.

A demolition foreman was removing asbestos cement roof sheets from a factory roof when he fell 7.5 m through the fragile roof to the concrete floor below. He received multiple injuries from which he died four weeks later. No equipment was provided on the roof to allow the work to be carried out safely.

Short-duration work

110 'Short-duration work' means tasks that are measured in minutes rather than hours. It includes tasks such as inspection, replacing a few tiles or minor adjustment to a television aerial. It may not be reasonably practicable to install safeguards such as a full independent scaffold or even edge protection for such work, but you will need to provide something in its place. The decision on the precautions to take will depend on an overall assessment of the risks involved. You should consider:

- duration of the work;
- complexity of the work;
- pitch of the roof;
- condition of the roof;
- type of roofing material (slate or tile);
- weather conditions;
- risk to those putting up edge protection; and
- risk to other workers and the public.

111 The minimum requirements for short-duration work on a roof are:

- a safe means of access to the roof level; and
- safe means of working on the roof, eg:
  - on a sloping roof, a properly constructed and supported roof ladder; or
  - on a flat roof without edge protection, a harness with a sufficiently short lanyard, attached to a secured anchorage, that it prevents the wearer from reaching a position from which they could fall.

112 Mobile access equipment or proprietary access systems can provide a suitable working platform in some situations and can be particularly appropriate for short-duration minor work (see Figure 16). Where this is not practicable, then work restraint or fall-arrest systems could be considered.

Figure 16 A mobile elevating work platform being used to replace a roof sheet

113 When using fall-protection systems for short-duration roof work, fall protection equipment (used as work restraint) is preferable to fall arrest, as it prevents people falling by physically restricting their movement to a safe area. It should not be possible to reach any unprotected edge, hole or fragile material when relying on this type of system.

114 Fall arrest is not the same as work restraint (see Figure 17). Fall arrest relies on minimising injury once a fall has occurred. In both cases, seek specialist advice on anchorage points from the equipment supplier. Supervision and training are needed to make sure that the system of work adopted is understood by all and is maintained. **A rescue plan is also necessary in the event that someone should fall.**

115 Harnesses need to be suitable for the individual, who should be trained to fit and use them. They only protect someone when they are properly fitted and only while they are attached to a suitable anchorage point. There must be enough clear space below the work position to allow the fall to be arrested safely (see Appendix 3). They are not an easy option. See paragraphs 45–51 and Appendices 2 and 3 for further information on fall arrest.

Figure 17 Work restraint harness used during short-term inspection on a flat roof (Image courtesy of Safesite Limited)

Types of roof

116 This section explains the hazards characteristic of different roof types and the precautionary measures required to deal with them.

Flat roofs

117 Flat roofs are generally accepted as being up to 10° in pitch and are usually waterproofed with a membrane such as felt.

118 On flat roofs, falls most frequently occur:

- from the edge of a completed roof;
- during surveying, inspection or construction;
- from the edge where work is being carried out;
- through openings or gaps; and
- through surfaces that are, or have become, fragile, eg strawboard, unfixed profiled, metal decking, or aged roof lights (see paragraphs 166–182 and Appendix 4).

119 Where the design of the roof does not provide permanent edge protection, such as solid parapet wall of at least 950 mm in height, temporary edge protection will be required (eg guard rails and toe boards – see Figure 18). These should, when erected:

- give protection for the full duration of the work;
- be strong and rigid enough to prevent people from falling and be able to withstand other loads likely to be placed on it;
- when fixed to a structure, the structure should be capable of supporting it; and
- be designed in such a way that it is not necessary to remove it to work at the edge of the roof.

Figure 18 Temporary flat-roof edge protection. Adjustable supports enable work to progress with protection in place (Image courtesy of Safesite Limited)

120 Guard rails should preferably be supported at ground level, if the height of the building allows, so they do not obstruct work on the roof edge (see Figure 19). For a higher structure, they can be supported by an upstand at the edge of the roof, if this is strong enough (see Figure 20). Guard rails can also be supported by frames, counterweights or scaffolding on the roof.

121 All guard rails should meet the minimum legal standard contained in the Work at Height Regulations 2005, ie they should include:

- a main guard rail at least 950 mm above any edge from which people are liable to fall;
- a toe board, which should be suitable and sufficient to prevent the fall of any person, material or object, usually at least 150 mm high; and
- an intermediate guard rail, barrier or suitable alternative, positioned so that the unprotected gap is no greater than 470 mm.

Demarcation of access routes and work areas

122 Where limited work is being carried out on sections of a large roof, and edge protection around the whole perimeter is not reasonably practicable, a simple form of continuous physical barrier some distance from the roof edge could identify the work area and any access route to it. The distance should be adequate to make sure that people working within the demarcated area cannot fall from the edge of the roof. Where this method is used on roofs with a slight slope, it may be necessary to prevent materials rolling away beyond the 'safe' area.

123 In most circumstances a distance of at least 2 m from the edge will be sufficient. This will depend on the geometry of the roof and may need to be increased. This type of barrier is only acceptable where there is a high level of supervision and discipline to make sure that people do not go beyond the demarcated area. There should be no unprotected holes, breaks or fragile material within the 'safe area'. If there are any, they should be protected with robust covers or continuous physical barriers. All barriers should be durable and immediately obvious to all. Bunting, tape or markings at foot level, such as a painted line, are not sufficient (see Figure 21).

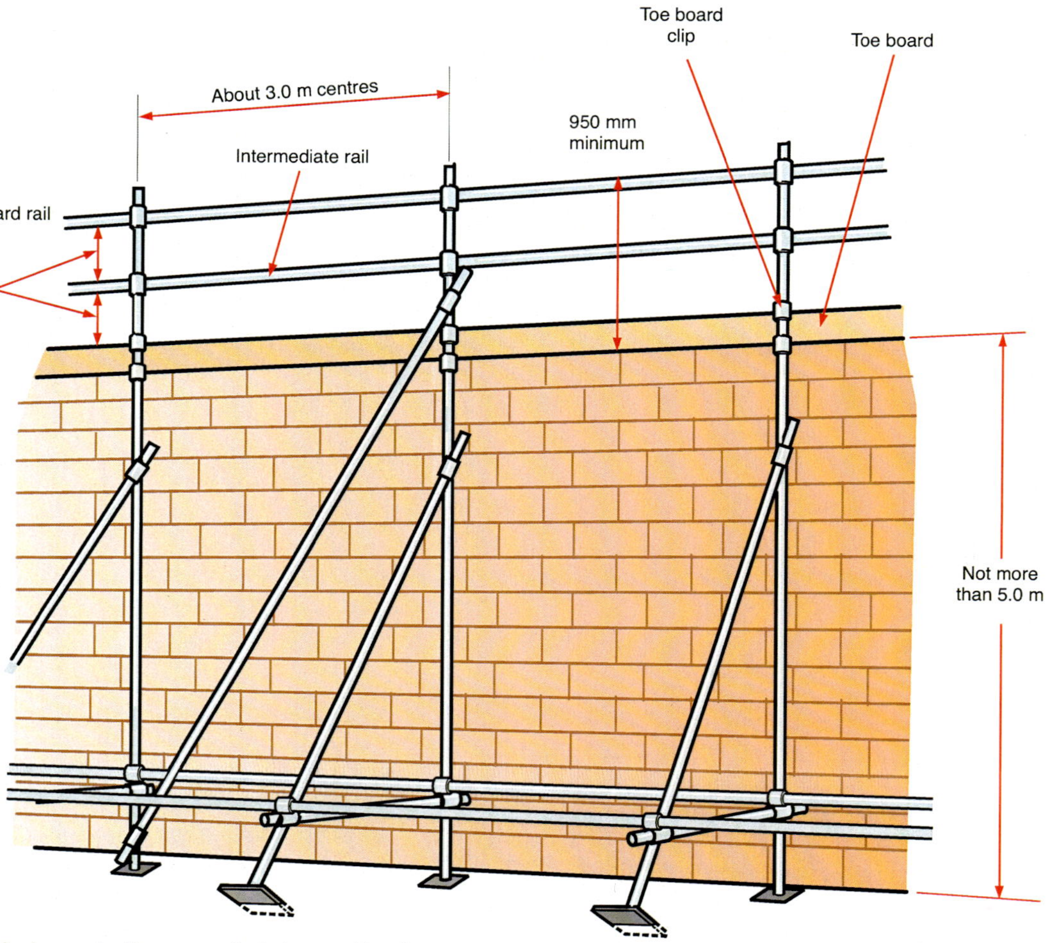

Figure 19 Flat-roof edge protection supported at ground level. Ground-level support allows work up to the roof edge without obstruction

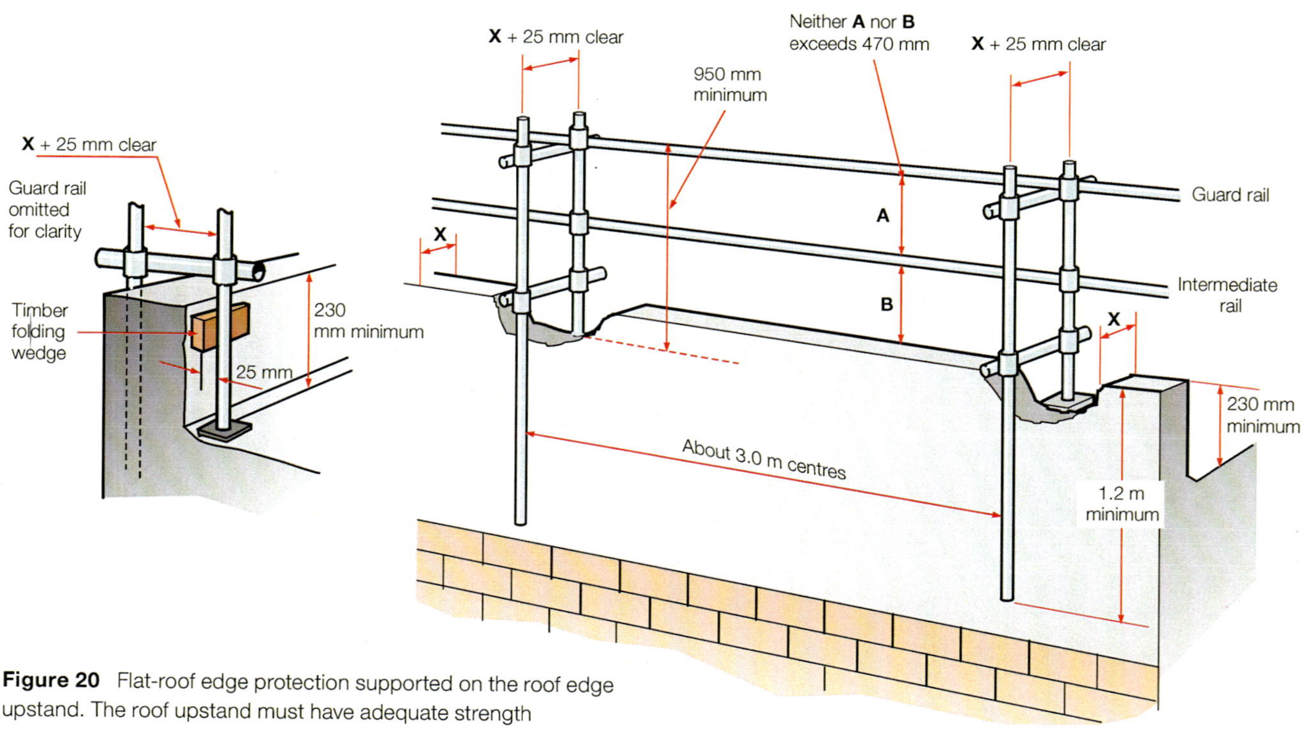

Figure 20 Flat-roof edge protection supported on the roof edge upstand. The roof upstand must have adequate strength

Figure 21 Demarcation barriers on a large, non-fragile roof, preventing access to the adjacent fragile roof lights. The roof lights are at least 2 m from the barrier

124 For short-duration work on flat roofs, it may not be feasible to provide edge protection. (See paragraphs 110–115 for further guidance on short-duration work.)

Slated and tiled roofs

125 On traditional pitched roofs, most falls occur:

- from the eaves;
- from the roof, typically slipping down the roof, then falling from the eaves;
- from the roof, falling internally, eg during roof truss erection, stripping roofs, installing membranes and re-roofing; and
- from gable ends.

126 To prevent falls, consider the following during design and installation of roofs:

- hoisting and lowering of materials;
- gaining access to and egress from roof level;
- falls from access platforms;
- gaining access to and egress from platform to roof;
- falls from eaves, between trusses and from the verge;
- transporting roof materials to roof area;
- laying felt/underlay and/or insulation;
- fixing battens, trusses, slates or tiles;
- loading out with slates or tiles;
- gaining access to the ridge after slates or tiles are fitted;
- transporting materials and mortar to the ridge;
- fixing the ridge; and
- securing fall-protection systems.

Roof truss erection

127 Prefabrication on the ground allows completed sections or whole roofs to be craned into place. This greatly reduces the need for work at height (see Figure 22). Where this is possible pre-assembly and mechanical lifting should be carried out. A safe working platform will be required around the perimeter of the building to fix the trusses into position on the wall plate.

Figure 22 Craning a pre-assembled roof into position greatly reduces the need for work at height (Image courtesy of the Trussed Rafter Association)

128 If prefabrication is not possible and trusses are assembled in situ, a safe working platform should be provided around the perimeter of the roof, and measures to prevent or mitigate the distance of a fall, should one occur, must also be provided internally. This can be achieved by providing a working platform or 'crash deck' immediately beneath the underside of the trusses. Either conventional scaffolding, or (if appropriate) proprietary decking systems can be used for this (see Figure 15(a)). Alternatively, if a platform cannot be provided, nets can be used if a safe clearance distance below the net and a suitable fixing point can be achieved. Alternatives to nets are soft landing systems such as bean or air bags (see Figure 15(b)–(c)).

129 Providing nets or soft landing systems is also particularly important when installing temporary or permanent bracing or before boarding out along the bottom chord of trusses when access is required within the trusses. Any equipment used to gain access to higher levels of the truss should be properly designed and stable.

130 Working platforms can be supported by the truss members if they are stable and capable of sustaining the load. Guard rails should be provided unless truss members provide a similar standard of protection. Work below should be prohibited unless workers are protected from falling materials (see Figure 23).

131 Systems such as nets or air and bean bags should only be relied on where a working platform to the standard described in paragraph 130 is not feasible. Where it is used:

- attachment points must be fit for purpose, eg where blockwork is used to support nets, time must be allowed for the mortar to cure and reach sufficient strength to sustain the load should a fall occur;
- the risk of injury during the fall, eg from striking parts of the rafters or blockwork, needs to be carefully assessed; and
- working platforms should be provided as far as reasonably practicable in addition to the measures taken to arrest a fall.

See Appendices 2 and 3 for further information.

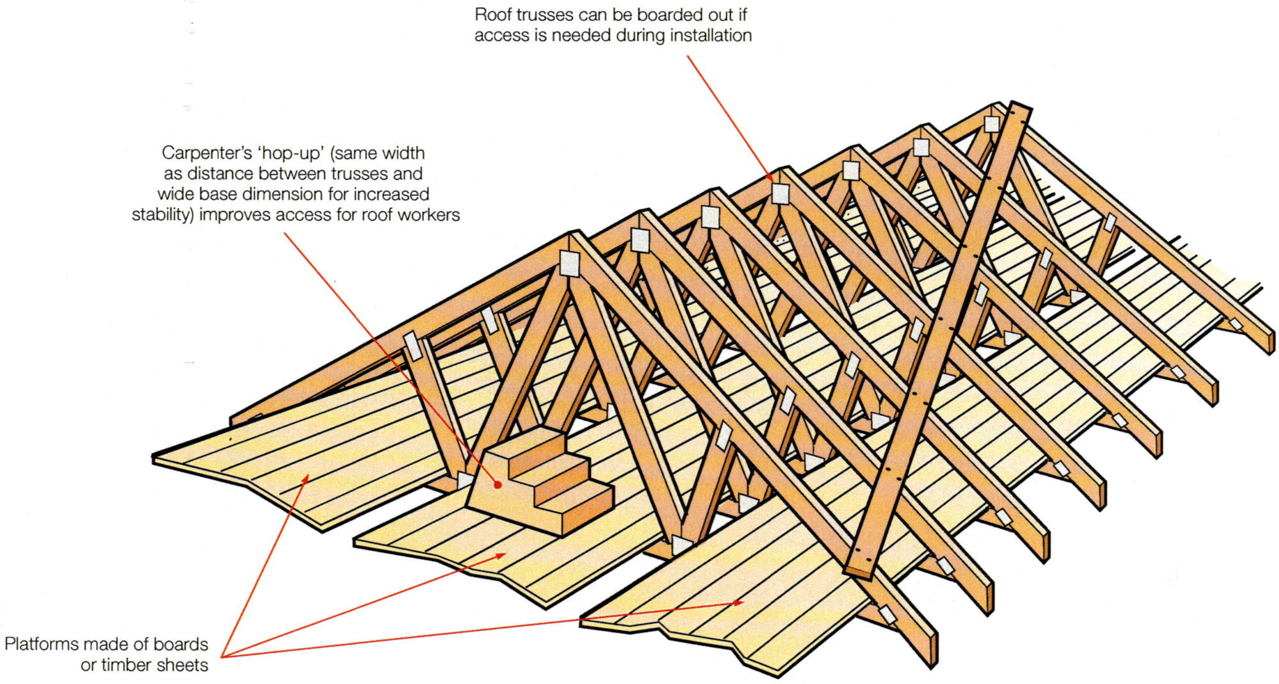

Figure 23 Roof trusses can be boarded out if access is needed during installation. Hop-up platforms improve access

132 Rafters and rafter bundles should be stored so that they will be stable under foreseeable conditions – see the *Trussed Rafter Association Technical Handbook*.[12] If they are to be stored on a scaffold, scaffold designers should be made aware of this so they can consider additional loading in the design. The scaffold platform can be extended to allow for safe storage and buttressing can be included to keep the trusses stable.

Handling roof trusses

133 Always use a crane or other mechanical handling device for lifting trusses, unless this is not reasonably practicable.

134 Good planning and design can avoid or reduce the need for manually handling roof trusses and this should be your aim. For instance, site layout designs can consider the need for crane locations. Work plans can then allow for cranage areas to be clear of other activities when trusses are installed.

135 Roof trusses can vary a great deal in size and shape. There are several configurations, eg attic, duo-pitched, single pitched, and laminated (or plied). Trusses can measure from a few metres wide and high to 20 m long and 5 m high.

136 Most fabricated trusses weigh below 75 kg, typically in the region of 50–70 kg. Some single trusses can weigh as much as 150 kg, and if plied together with another, up to about 200 kg. Attic (or 'room in roof') trusses are particularly heavy – they have large timber members to make up for the lack of triangulation timbers.

137 Trusses should be mechanically handled. However, where this is not possible, you should introduce measures to reduce the risks of musculoskeletal injury associated with manually handling roof trusses in teams. Use the following recommendations:

- manual handling should **not** be used for structures more than two storeys high;
- the area where the trusses are carried should be kept clear. Stockpiles of wood or other obstructions should not be present where team members may have to step across or around to complete the task;
- operatives should not jump or step from level to level while supporting a truss; and
- efforts should be made to reduce general noise levels so team members communicate more effectively and are better able to co-ordinate the handling task.

138 When handling the truss, enough team members will be needed on each level that the truss is raised to. Sufficient room is needed on each level for the members of the team and the truss. No member of the handling team should be exposed to the risk of a fall.

139 When truss handling in teams, there are risks of over exertion and cumulative musculoskeletal disorder (MSD). There is also a risk of an accident as co-ordination within the team operation is vital. With team lifts, there is a chance that co-ordination and therefore control over the load could be lost.

140 If manual handling is the only option, you should have a safe system of work (see Figure 24). A method statement, specific instruction and training will be required to make sure all handlers understand their role in the operation.

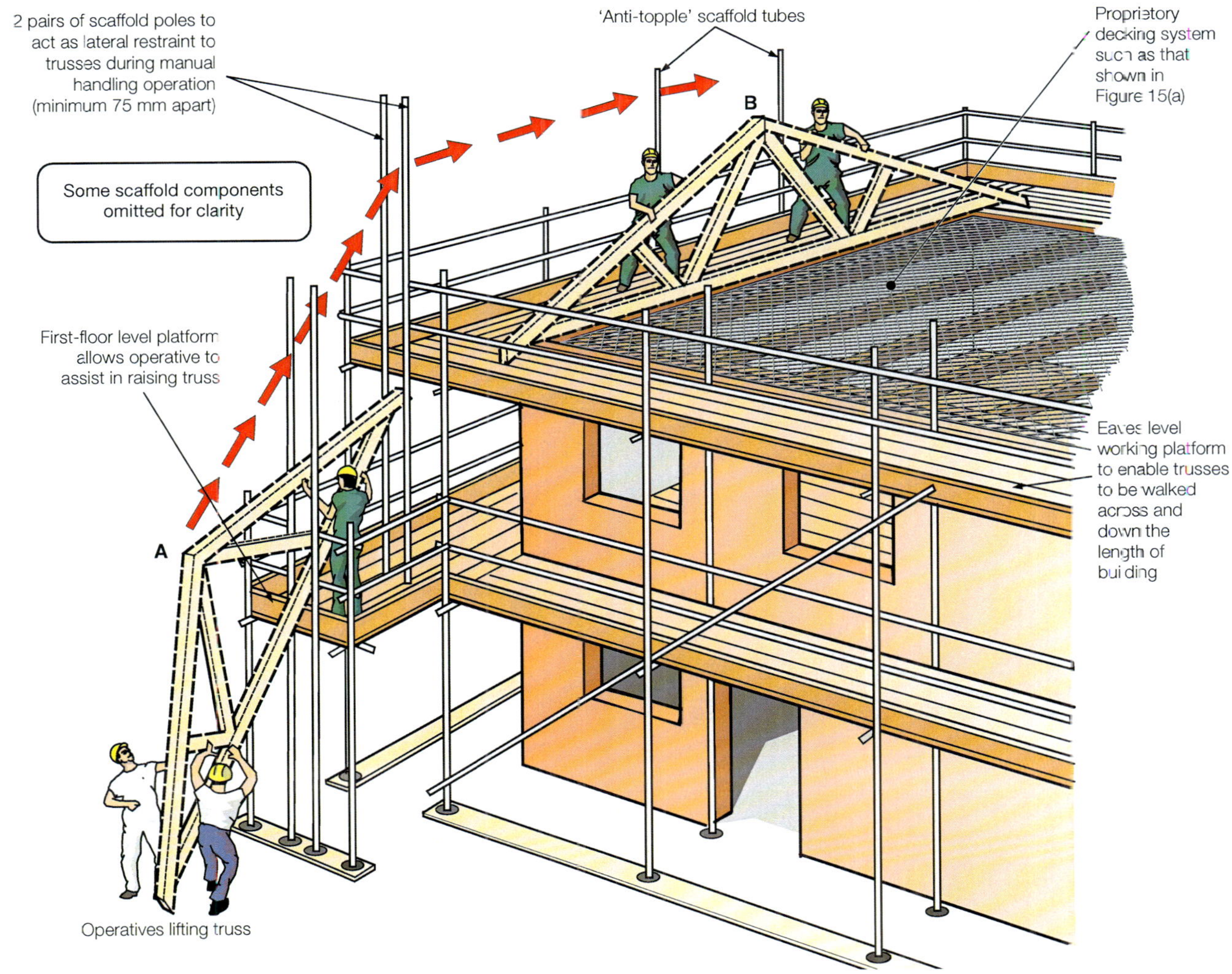

Figure 24 Suggested method for manual lifting of trusses to eaves level

141 Trusses over 95 kg should not be handled by manual means alone. Some form of mechanisation or mechanical assistance should also be used.

142 Remember – it really is best if the trusses can be mechanically handled.

143 Work programming should include enough time for the supporting structure to gain sufficient strength before roof construction begins, eg blockwork should be adequately cured. Gable walls are usually unstable until tied into the roof assembly and can collapse during truss erection. Unless steps are taken to ensure stability, gable walls should be completed after the trussed rafter roof construction. Party wall construction in terraced units should follow the same principle unless temporary restraint is provided. Safe access for the bricklayers will need to be planned in for any work that cannot be done from the eaves scaffold.

144 Roof designers can contribute substantially to safe working. For example, they can design temporary and permanent bracing which can be fitted from a safe place (see paragraphs 336–350).

Open rafters

145 You must consider and address the risk of falling through the open rafters when fixing tile support systems or when laying underlay and fixing battens.

146 This is achieved by following the work at height hierarchy and putting in place measures that prevent a fall where it is reasonably practicable to do so. Where it is not reasonably practicable to prevent a fall, you must provide measures that mitigate the distance and consequences of a fall.

147 What is reasonably practicable will differ between new-build properties and strip and re-cover roofing jobs. Some examples of reasonably practicable measures include:

- boarding out the inside of the roof using timber (see Figure 23);
- using proprietary decking systems (see Figure 15(a));
- inserting air bags or bean bags (see Figures 15(b) and (c))
- installing a safety net; or
- using boards in conjunction with a safe system of work.

Please note the above list is not exhaustive.

148 Falls from sloping roofs are more likely if the pitch is steep, if the surface is slippery and in windy conditions. Moisture, ice, snow, moss and lichens all increase the risk of slipping (see paragraphs 63–68).

149 For work on sloping roofs, unless of very short duration, full edge protection (as described in paragraph 151) is required on all roof elevations to which access is needed. This is to prevent people and materials falling from the lower edge of the roof. The potential loading on edge protection when a person slides down a pitched roof onto it is much greater than when falling against it on a flat roof. Make sure that the scaffold supplier knows the roof pitch when you specify edge protection.

150 If work on the roof requires access within 2 m of gable ends, then edge protection will be needed at those edges. At gable ends there should be one or more working platforms between the eaves height and the ridge. The distance from the highest working platform to the ridge should be no more than one lift high.

151 A scaffold platform at eaves level provides a good standard of edge protection, a working platform and storage space for materials (see Figure 25(b)). The working platform should be as close as possible to the eaves and is recommended to be no greater than 300 mm below eaves level. Brick guards will be necessary if materials, eg roof slates, are stacked above toe board height. They can also reduce gaps between guard rails, but need to be designed for this purpose (taking account of the pitch of the roof) and securely fixed.

152 Where independent scaffold edge protection is not practicable, barriers can be attached to the structure instead; Figure 25(a) shows an example. The barriers must be high enough (probably greater than the 950 mm minimum to allow for a person standing on a rising slope) and strong enough to stop someone who has lost their balance and who may walk/run uncontrolled, roll or slide down a roof slope. The strength and spacing of the guard rails, or gaps in the edge protection, should conform to BS EN 13374. For edge protection to roof slopes greater than 10° these spaces and gaps are significantly less than 470 mm (see Appendix 7).

153 With some long, steeply sloping roofs, edge protection may prevent a fall from eaves level, but it may not prevent serious injury if a roof worker falls from a position high on the roof slope. Additional precautions may be required, eg intermediate platforms at the work site or work platforms cantilevered out from an independent scaffold. If this is not practicable, then safety harnesses may be appropriate (see Appendix 3). In all cases, the edge protection should be designed to minimise injury as well as to prevent a further fall. Safety netting can be incorporated into edge protection

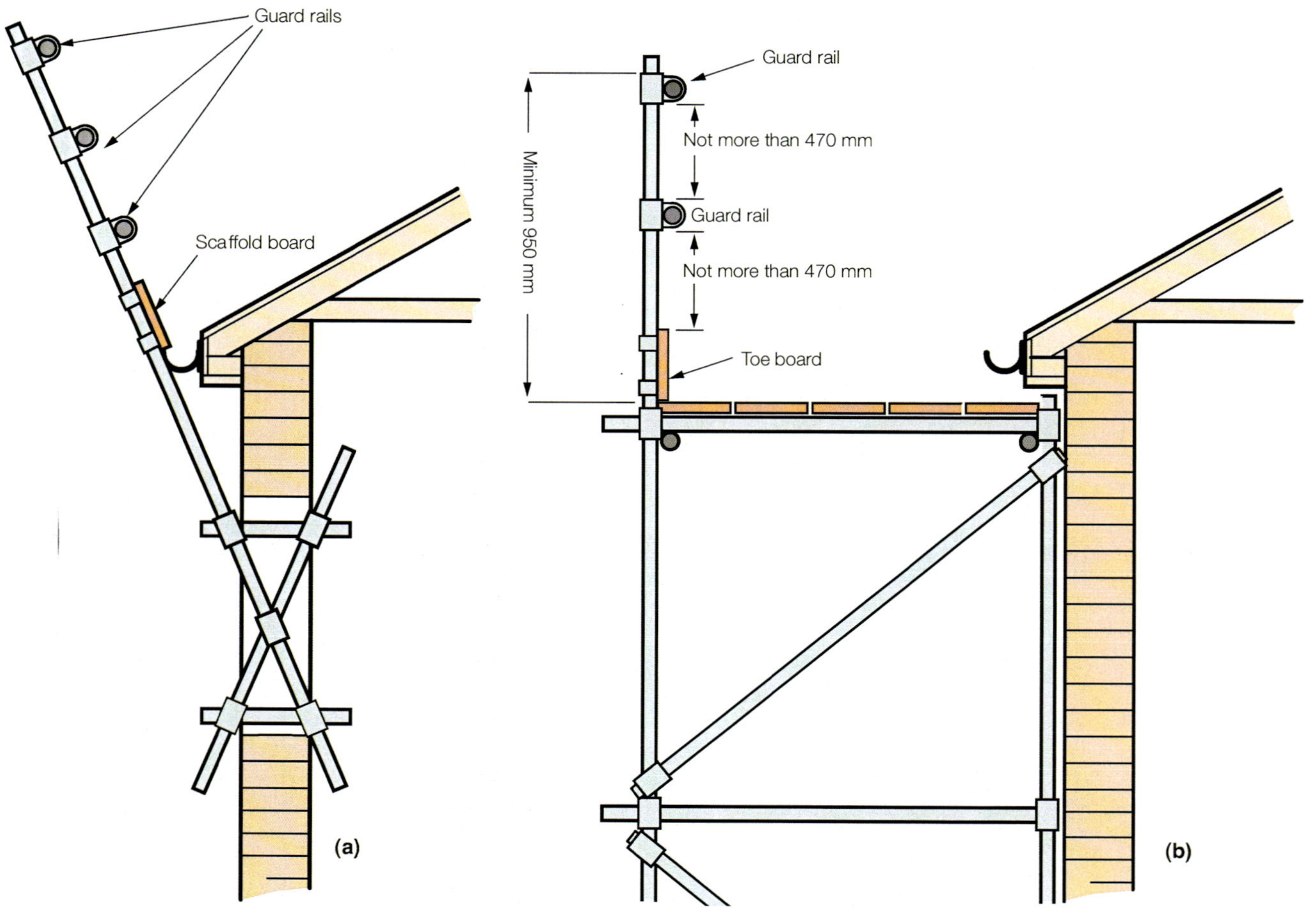

Figure 25 Typical sloping roof edge protection. If using edge protection placed directly at the bottom of a roof slope, as in (a), you must ensure spacing between guard rails and the performance of the edge protection conforms with BS EN 13374 (see Appendix 7) and guard rails are high enough to allow for a person on the rising roof slope

to absorb some of the energy of impact and some netting products are specifically designed to act as edge protection.

154 For short-duration work on a pitched roof (eg replacing a few tiles or slates) the decision on whether or not to erect edge protection will depend on a number of factors (see paragraphs 110–115).

155 The minimum standard for short-duration work on a pitched roof is:

- safe means of access to roof level; and
- a properly constructed and supported roof ladder (see paragraphs 160–165) or equivalent.

156 Roof workers should not work directly on tiles or slates unless additional measures are provided to prevent falls, eg a roof ladder, or if this is not possible, a safety harness with a suitable anchorage point.

157 Roofers should avoid walking on the roof coverings and should slate or tile the roofs in such a way that the battens always support them. The practice of walking on roof coverings was and still is commonplace on slated roofs and/or steep roofs – it should be avoided on all roofs because tile/slate roof coverings are not designed to be walked on and offer no firm footholds. This will mean bringing valleys, ridge and hip tiles through as the roof is covered and working in a planned way to cut down foot traffic on the finished roof. This is especially important in light of the new zonal fixing method (see Figure 26), as it will mean that every tile will have to be nailed as a minimum for most roofs, so pushing tiles up and/or replacing tiles broken by foot traffic will not be as simple.

Slating direct to boarded roofs

158 For many years the use of metal 'spikes' or 'heels' has been an integral part of Scottish practice. It is still quite common to fix slates straight to boards, which means there are no battens to be used as footholds. The metal 'spikes' are driven into the roof and are used as hop-ups by the roofers. For more information on this see NFRC website (www.nfrc.co.uk) and Information Sheet *Slater's heel.*[13]

Chimney scaffolds

159 For work on chimneys, a properly designed chimney scaffold should be used (see Figures 27 and 28), unless the work can be done from a sitting/horizontal position on a cat ladder, such as pointing or lead inspection.

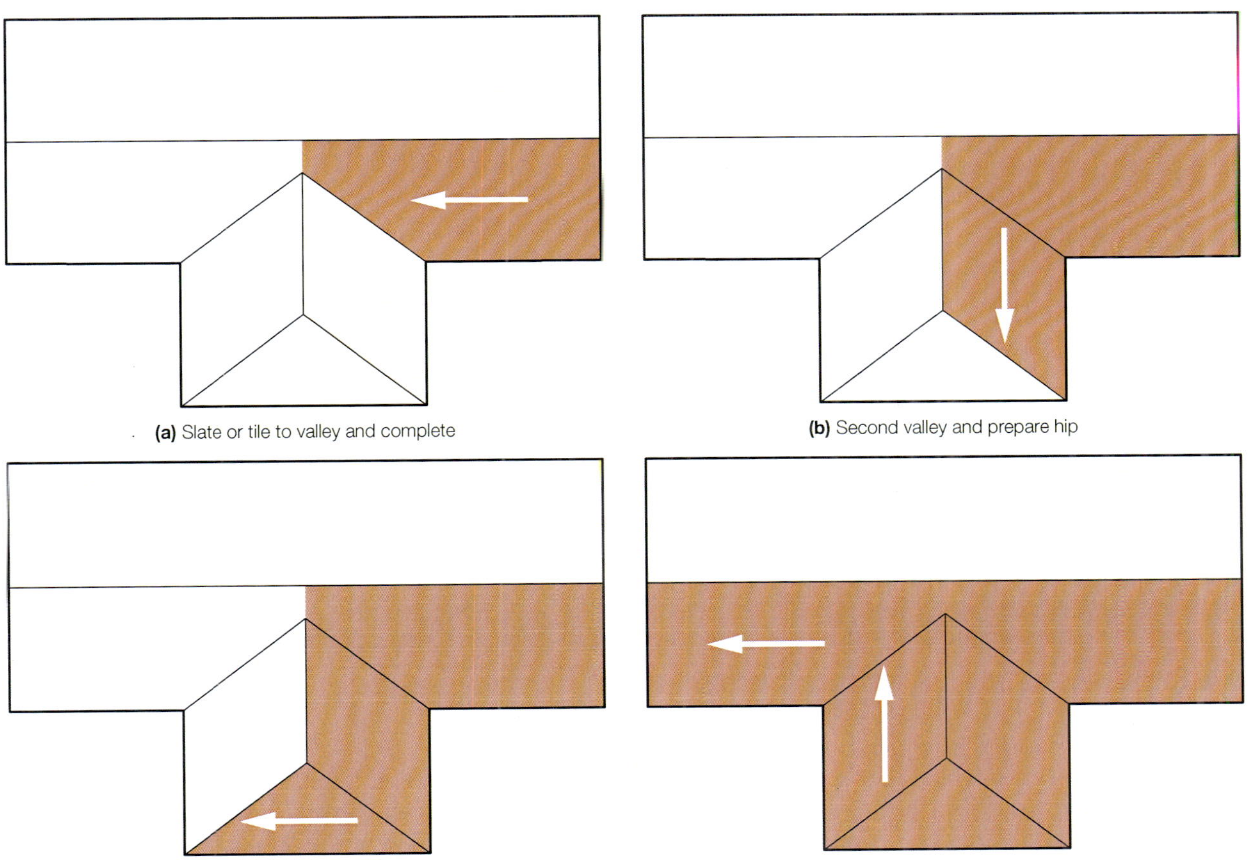

(a) Slate or tile to valley and complete

(b) Second valley and prepare hip

(c) Bring hip up with slating/tiling

(d) Continue as before, bringing the main ridge through

(e) The roof is completed by bringing through the ridge tiles as the back is covered

Figure 26 Example of directional working on battens

Figure 27 A traditional chimney scaffold

Figure 28 Proprietary system for access to roof and chimney

Roof ladders

160 On most sloping roofs, suitable roof ladders or crawling boards will be essential, **in addition to** edge protection. Where a high standard of edge protection is provided, it **may** be safe to work without a roof ladder. This may apply if the pitch is shallow and the surface provides particularly good foothold and is non-fragile. In each case the decision should be based on a risk assessment.

161 Roof ladders or crawling boards should be:

- designed and fabricated to be fit for purpose;
- strong enough to support workers when spanning across the supports for the roof covering;
- long enough to span the supports (at least three rafters); and
- secured or placed to prevent accidental movement.

162 The anchorage at the top of the roof ladder should be by some method which does not depend on the ridge capping as this is liable to break away from the ridge. The anchorage should bear on the opposite slope by a properly designed and manufactured ridge hook (see Figure 29) or be secured by other means.

Figure 29 Roof ladder. The ridge iron should be large enough to be clear of the ridge tile

A 34-year-old self-employed roofer fell from the edge of a pitched roof to a two-storey house when his home-made roof ladder slid down the roof. He was replacing chimney pots and an access scaffold was in position, but only a single guard rail was fitted and he slid beneath this to his death.

163 Eaves gutters should not be used as a footing or to support a roof ladder unless they are of adequate strength – this is not usually the case. Gutters normally used on houses are not suitable.

164 Where slated and tiled roofs are being covered, timber battens can provide a reasonably secure foothold provided that the following criteria are adhered to:

- the battens are fixed to rafters set at centres not more than 600 mm apart;
- the battens are a minimum size of 50 mm x 25 mm and meet the grading requirements specified in BS 5534:2003+A1:2010 *Code of practice for slating and tiling (including shingles)*[14] and NFRC Technical Bulletin 33 *Graded battens for slating and tiling*;[15]
- the battens are at least 1.2 m long to ensure they span a minimum of three trusses;
- the battens are only fixed with the recommended nails;
- the safe system of work dictates that the roofers never deliberately walk on the battens mid-span between the trusses; and
- the safe system of work dictates that the roofers always walk on the rafter line when installing the tiles and slates.

165 A roof ladder will always be required at some stage, eg towards the end of the job when the battens are covered by tiles.

A 50-year-old roofer was killed when he fell from the edge of a pitched roof. He was understood to have been carrying out extensive work to repair the roof following storm damage. There was no edge protection and the access ladder was not secured.

A self-employed roofer aged 29 was killed when he fell from the edge of a pitched roof. He was repointing a chimney stack and replacing some tiles on the roof and gained access using an extending ladder/roof ladder. However, there was no roof ladder on the rear elevation and he fell from the edge of the pitched roof at the rear of the property.

Fragile roofs

166 Falls through fragile surfaces account for 22% of all the fatal accidents which result from a fall from height in the construction industry. However, deaths caused by falls through fragile surfaces don't just occur in the construction industry; those working in the maintenance sector are also affected and this involves a whole range of fragile surfaces.

167 The terms 'fragility' and 'fragile surfaces' are used in this book to describe roof assemblies that will not safely support the weight of a person and any materials they may be carrying.

168 The test to show non-fragility for a roofing assembly has been drawn up by the Advisory Committee for Roofsafety (ACR) and is published in *Test for non-fragility of roofing assemblies*.[16] The test is discussed in greater detail in Appendix 4.

169 All designers and contractors should make sure that any non-fragile roof assemblies they design or fix have been tested in accordance with the above standard and are classified non-fragile Class 'C' as a minimum for low-maintenance roofs, and Class 'B' for medium-maintenance roofs. Refer to the ACR best-practice guide *Recommended practice for work on profiled sheeted roofs*[17] for more information.

170 Whatever roofing assembly has been specified, all non-fragile roofs will deteriorate with time and at some point the assembly will become fragile. All roofs, once fixed, should be treated as fragile until a competent person has confirmed that they are non-fragile.

171 In particular, the following are likely to be fragile:

- old roof lights;
- old liner panels on built-up sheeted roofs;
- non-reinforced fibre cement sheets;
- corroded metal sheets, either as the primary waterproofing system or as the structural deck supporting a membrane roofing system;
- glass (including wired glass);
- rotted chipboard or similar;
- wood wool slabs; and
- slates and tiles.

172 Falls through fragile materials are a particular problem in both the roof work and building maintenance sectors. Everyone with responsibility for this type of work, at whatever level, should treat falls as a priority. This is particularly important for small, short-term maintenance and cleaning jobs. See ACR guidance note *Safe working on fragile roofs*.[18]

A 60-year-old employee was killed when he fell through a fragile roof as he was helping to install a ventilation duct for a spray booth.

A self-employed builder, aged 52, fell while he was trying to repair damage to the asbestos cement roof of an industrial unit. He fell through a fragile roof light.

173 Fragile roof accidents are not inevitable. They can be prevented by careful planning, using suitable equipment and employing a high level of supervision.

174 If possible, arrange the work to avoid working on or passing near fragile material. If this is unavoidable, you should identify all fragile materials and put precautions in place to prevent or minimise the effects of a fall. This applies to all operations on the roof, whether construction, maintenance, repair, cleaning or demolition.

175 The hierarchy for work on fragile roofs is:

- work from underneath the roof using a suitable work platform;
- where this is not possible, consider using a MEWP that allows people to work from within the MEWP basket without standing on the roof itself;
- if access onto the fragile roof cannot be avoided, perimeter edge protection should be installed and staging used to spread the load. Unless all the work and access is on staging or platforms that are fitted with guard rails, safety nets should be installed underneath the roof or a harness system used; and
- where harnesses are used they need adequate anchorage points. They also rely on discipline, training and supervision to make sure that they are used consistently and correctly.

176 Some roof coverings can give a false sense of security to those who are working on or passing by them. They may be capable of carrying some distributed load, giving the impression that they can bear a person's weight, but they might not carry a concentrated load, eg the heel of someone walking or someone stumbling and falling. A stumble may cause the roof to fail instantly like a trap door. For example, asbestos cement and other non-reinforced fibre cement sheeting are liable to shatter without warning under a stumble. They will also become more brittle with age.

177 A common but fatal belief persists that it is safe to walk along the line of the roof bolts above the purlins. In practice this could be the weakest part of the roof:

- some roofing sheets (eg roof lights, asbestos cement and fibre cement) have their weakest point of impact within 150 mm of the purlin line since the purlin provides an edge to tear the sheets; and
- on occasion, the original sheets are of a length so that the sheet end overlap does not coincide with the purlin line. When this occurs, and to avoid end lap leaking, the end laps are stitched together using simple bolts. To the unwary, this appears to be the line of a purlin, when in fact there is no support underneath at all.

178 So walking the purlins is walking a tightrope: one false step or loss of balance can lead to disaster. Do **not** assume that double-skin roofs are safe – each layer can fail independently.

179 Roof lights discolour with age. They may have been painted to reduce glare, making them difficult to identify. In some cases, insulation may have been applied externally to a roof that is generally load bearing but contains fragile roof lights; this can obscure the roof lights. Roof surveyors should look for signs of repair etc (see Figure 30).

Figure 30 In some light conditions, it is difficult to distinguish the roof lights from the metal sheets on this type of roof. The valley gutter is very narrow and roof lights extend down to gutter level. Both of these features increase the risk during cleaning, maintenance or refurbishment

A labourer cleaning a gutter was seriously injured when he fell 9 m after stepping onto a roof light.

180 If any material is applied that may disguise fragile parts of a roof, the fragile parts should be clearly marked and the information recorded. It should be included in any health and safety file for the building or any permit-to-work system for the roof. Warning notices should be erected at all access points (see paragraphs 197–198).

181 Wood wool slabs may fracture beneath someone's weight. You should treat the following as fragile:

- wood wool slabs less than 75 mm thick without a nylon net reinforcement;
- wood wool slabs with a nylon net reinforcement but less than 50 mm thick;
- wood wool slabs that are wet or previously damaged;
- all straw boards, but especially those affected by water; and
- all slabs where it is not possible to determine either their condition or the specific type that has been used.

182 In some situations the structure supporting the roof covering may deteriorate so much that the roof becomes 'fragile' and could fail catastrophically. In such a situation a thorough survey is essential.

Preventing falls through fragile material

183 Carefully consider whether the task warrants the risk involved in working at height on a fragile roof assembly. Can the work be avoided? Or can you provide a better job and longer-term solution by:

- over-roofing or re-roofing with a non-fragile assembly, instead of multiple repairs that may fail in the short term;
- replacing sheets, instead of using patch repairs; or
- where practical, replacing roof lights from below, using a proprietary replacement and fixing system.

184 Always make sure that the workers carrying out the tasks on the fragile roof are adequately supervised and trained, understand and follow the method statement they will be working to and have a thorough knowledge of the materials, equipment and tools they will be using.

185 A safe working platform on the roof and safe access to the working position must be provided when working on fragile roofs:

- platforms or coverings spanning the purlins must be provided and used to support the weight of anyone on the fragile material; and
- guard rails or coverings are required to prevent someone who is passing or working near fragile material from falling through.

186 The platforms or covering must be adequately secured against slippage.

187 Boundaries can be established identifying 'safe' areas containing the workplace and routes to and from it. If these are used:

- the boundary should be at least 2 m from the nearest fragile material;
- the boundary does not need to comply with full edge protection standards, but there should be a continuous physical barrier (a painted line or bunting is not acceptable); and
- tight discipline is essential to make sure that everyone stays within the safe area at all times.

188 Stagings of a suitable and sufficient width fitted with guard rails meeting the standard in paragraph 121 can be used where the roof pitch permits. The roof structure needs to be strong enough to take the combined weight of the staging, guard rails, workers and any materials or equipment used. There should be enough stagings available to allow the work to be carried out safely. Workers should not have to move stagings continually to progress over the roof. Stagings should also be long enough to provide adequate support across roof members. They should span across at least two purlins.

189 In most situations additional measures (usually in the form of fall arrest such as safety nets or harnesses and running line systems) are required to protect those using trolley systems from falling through a gap created when replacing an old sheet or roof light.

190 Where it is not practicable to maintain guard rails on both sides of the staging, other collective fall protection measures will be required, eg:

- birdcage scaffolds;
- MEWPs;
- mobile towers or scaffold used as a crash deck;
- safety nets (as long as there is adequate clearance below) (see Figure 31); and
- a soft landing system.

These give the most freedom to workers on the roof and can protect people working below, such as during a refurbishment project, particularly if debris netting is also used (see Appendix 2).

191 Harness and line systems can also form part of the system of work but they are lower down the hierarchy for work at height as they rely on operator training and a high level of supervision. The quality of the attachment system is critical. There are also minimum heights below which the system will be ineffective; in this case, someone may hit the floor before the restraint is fully operational. See Appendix 3 for further guidance.

Figure 31 Safety netting used to provide protection for roof lights during minor roof works

192 Make sure that at all times the work area is clean and tidy to avoid slips and trips which may lead to falls.

193 Where a valley or parapet gutter is used for access it should be of a suitable width and of sufficient strength. Take precautions to prevent anyone falling from any edge or through fragile material in an adjacent roof. Where access along gutters is necessary on a regular (even if infrequent) basis, then permanent protection should be provided. Where practicable, this should provide collective rather than individual protection. Fixed covers, for example, are preferable to running line systems (see Figure 32).

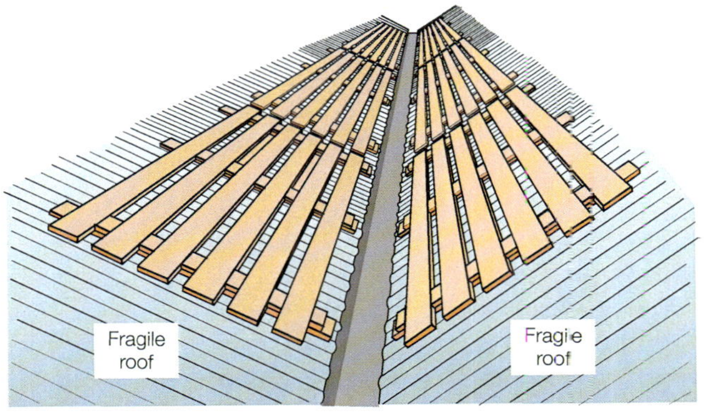

Figure 32 Permanent protection installed at valley gutter. (The protection should be supported by at least three rafters beneath the roof sheets)

194 Covers should be fitted far enough up the roof to protect anyone who falls against them. This is normally up to 2 m, depending on the roof pitch; shallower pitches will need more extensive coverage than steeper ones. Remember that protection (such as safety nets or a birdcage scaffold) is needed when covers are being installed. Valley gutters that are overhung by roof sheets so much that there is not enough space for someone's feet should not be used for access along the roof. It should be possible to clean the gutters without removing walkways or covers.

195 Roof lights should not extend within 2 m of valley gutters. Where fragile roof lights have already been fitted in this position and access is needed, consider permanently protecting the roof lights. See Figure 32.

196 Take precautions to prevent unauthorised access to fragile roofs. This will normally involve people at work, but you may also need to consider the likelihood of unauthorised public access, particularly by children (see *Protecting the public: Your next move* HSG151[19]). A risk assessment made under the Management of Health and Safety at Work Regulations 1999 is likely to require signs warning of the hazard and prohibiting access except under controlled conditions, eg governed by a permit-to-work regime. Permanently fixed ladders can be blocked off by boards whenever access is not required.

197 Figure 33 illustrates a suitable sign which should be fixed at the approaches to roofs with fragile coverings. Such signs should be durable, securely fastened and properly maintained. Any signs used should meet the requirements of the Health and Safety (Safety Signs and Signals) Regulations 1996.[20]

198 Such signs are not an alternative to a designer's duty to design-out hazards at source. Their function is to warn of dangers on existing buildings and where the load-bearing properties of the roof assembly are either classed as fragile or are unclear because of ageing etc.

Figure 33 Typical fragile material warning sign

Profiled sheeting

199 This section deals with all roof work that uses large-element profiled sheeting, which typically will be industrial, large retail, commercial, sports complex and agricultural buildings.

200 The roofing system will generally be on a pitched roof of the following typical construction:

- built-up on-site assembly of liner, insulation and outer sheet;
- factory-assembled composite panel and laid as single unit; or
- single-skin application for unheated buildings.

201 The large-element sheeting will be fixed to steel or timber purlins.

202 Properly erected safety nets should be the preferred solution in conjunction with edge protection around the perimeter of the roof. When using nets, additional leading edge protection (this is not edge protection on the perimeter of the building – it is protection at the moving edge of the work area) will not normally be required.

Design issues

203 Designers need to consider the following three factors which will influence safety during construction, maintenance and demolition phases of profile sheet roofs:

- **non-fragility:** most industrial-grade profiled sheets, including roof lights, are now available to achieve a non-fragile status when installed. Designers should make sure that such specifications are followed during procurement and construction. A reduction in the thickness of the profiled sheeting, to save on cost, may result in a non-fragile specification becoming a fragile construction;
- **longevity:** whatever roofing assembly has been specified, all non-fragile roofs will deteriorate with time, and at some point the assembly will become fragile. Designers should therefore determine the design life of the roof and specify the roofing materials that will provide non-fragility for this period. Such information must be included in the health and safety file for the building. Environmental issues may also affect longevity;
- **material weight:** with an increasing need to provide better-insulated and more airtight buildings there is a growing need for thicker, longer and therefore heavier roof panels. Designers must consider the safety issues with handling the materials that they specify.

Systems of work

204 Falls from profiled sheeted roofs commonly occur:

- through roofing that is or has become fragile;
- through gaps in partially completed roofs;
- through lining panels that were not designed to be non-fragile as a single underlay;
- through sheeting that is not fully fixed;
- from the leading/working edge or gable edge and gutter; and
- when loading out the roof.

205 The system of work needs to include all stages of the job, including delivery of materials (see Appendix 1). Simply loading out the frame with packs of sheets, as delivered, leads to workers travelling around the roof, passing open edges more often, to get the correct length of sheet or accessories.

206 Ways of minimising travel on the roof include:

- using hoists to deliver materials to the working position or to loading bays;
- providing access points convenient to the working positions;
- splitting packs of roof sheets to produce mixed packs in the correct sequence for fixing; and
- back-loading sheets onto the completed (load-bearing) sections of roof.

See Figures 34 and 35.

Figure 34 Delivering sheets to roof level onto the completed load-bearing section and behind the leading edge. (Note that the roof lights include mesh protection and are non-fragile)

Figure 35 Loading bays should be designed for the actual weight of the materials to be placed on them and include an additional allowance for impact loads from mechanical handling (eg cranes or forklifts). A notice should clearly display the safe working load

207 Safe working positions and the means of access to and from those positions should be planned in advance. Remember to include people who accept and unsling loads and who deliver sheets to the working position. For example:

- provide working platforms on the roof, fitted with guard rails and toe boards;
- use mobile access equipment;
- use safety nets; and
- use suitable safety harnesses together with suitable anchorage points.

208 It is **not** acceptable for open steelwork or gutters to be used as the access route or place of work.

209 The weight of material should be limited to the amount that the structure can carry safely. Metal z-section purlins can twist and collapse under heavy loading. Sheets should be lashed to prevent them being dislodged or blown away. If necessary, use stops to prevent them slipping.

210 Falls from the edge of the building frame can be prevented by fitting edge protection. This is usually provided by an independent scaffold around the perimeter of the building or by barriers connected to a frame. **Barriers connected to the frame should conform to BS EN 13374**, see Appendix 7. An independent scaffold gives a higher standard of protection and a good standard of access along the structure. It also helps with material loading and storage, eg when used with a forklift/telehandler. In certain circumstances, proprietary net barrier systems can be used to provide fall arrest protection at edges where it is not reasonably practicable to provide conventional guard rails and/or barriers (see Figure 36).

Figure 36 Net barrier system

211 All profiled sheeting should be specified to be non-fragile when fully fixed. Contractors need to be aware that unfixed or partially fixed materials cause the roof assembly to be deemed fragile. Therefore, carefully developed systems of work must remain in place, including working edge protection and being fully netted out underneath

212 Lining out the roof as quickly as possible to 'weatherproof' the shell means that roof workers have to return in a second pass to lay the insulation and top sheets if composite panels are in use. Principal contractors should consider how this approach affects safe systems of work. If it is used, clarify the specification of metal and roof-light liners in terms of temporary fragility. The use of 'man safe' or 'walkable' non-fragile liners should be encouraged. Other resources may be needed to achieve a safe system of work, eg safety nets.

A roofer, aged 49, was killed when he fell through the fragile inner lining of an industrial roof where some steel roofing sheets had been removed. He was working to progressively replace the roof sheets and roof lights on the roof when he stepped on the open section of the lining and fell through as he attempted to avoid a roof light panel in the vicinity.

213 Falls through gaps, eg for smoke vents, are a common cause of serious injuries and death. Designers can help by eliminating or reducing the number of openings. If there is a need for openings in the roof, the use of safety nets should be considered at the tender stage to protect both the gaps and the leading (working) edge.

Leading edge protection

214 Take precautions to prevent falls from roof edges and working ('leading') edges. Nets and birdcage scaffolds are the preferred options. However, where these are not reasonably practicable you can consider using work-restraint safety harnesses with running line systems, or temporary barriers at the leading edge, eg trolley systems.

215 The preferred solution is to use properly erected safety nets along with edge protection around the perimeter of the roof. Nets give roof workers maximum freedom of movement, provided that they do not work beyond their boundary. They can be installed to minimise fall distances (see Appendix 2). They are effective where design details such as hips make other systems complex and difficult to manage. In a fall the chance of injury is reduced, compared to a similar fall in a harness or onto a birdcage scaffold. Nets protect the leading edge and gaps, fragile areas, etc (see Figure 36).

216 When using nets, additional leading edge protection will not usually be required.

217 The Advisory Committee on Roofsafety gives guidance on the safe use of nets in its blue book *Recommended practice for the use of safety nets for roof work.*[21]

218 Where it is not possible to use nets, other fall-arrest systems may be used. Running lines designed to be used with a suitable harness/lanyard can be attached to the structure, to a mobile anchor point or to a working platform. Running line systems should be designed and tested to make sure that they are fit for purpose. The quality of the attachment point is critical, as is the type of harness (belts are not acceptable for fall arrest). See Appendix 3 for further information.

219 Where a running line is attached to the structure, seek advice from the equipment supplier and the structural designer to make sure that the imposed loads can be sustained. Where it is attached to a working platform, the platform must be secured against overturning. Where a mobile anchor or inertial reel system is used, minimise the number of workers approaching the leading edge to reduce the risk of tripping and snagging.

220 **Remember** that most inertia reel devices are designed for use only where the anchor point is directly above the user, ie in the vertical plane. This is to avoid problems such as poor inertia reel performance (allowing freefall to occur), the lifeline shearing over an edge, or pendulum swing. Therefore their safe application could be limited.

221 **In any case** personal fall-protection systems should **not** be your first choice when considering how to avoid risk from work at height. Avoidance, fall prevention (guard rails, MEWPs, scaffolds etc), collective safeguards for arresting falls (nets, airbags, mats etc) and work-restraint systems should be considered first. See Figure 37.

222 Temporary barriers will be needed to control access to areas where harnesses have to be worn. Where running line systems are used, strictly control access to the roof, eg during work breaks and at the end of the working day.

Figure 37 Use of safety nets during industrial roof work

223 Temporary leading edge devices (eg purlin trolleys) are available and if locked in position they can provide an effective guard rail at the leading edge when work is not in progress. The disadvantage is that installing and moving the systems can be a high-risk operation. When used as a working platform, they often (in practice) provide little protection while laying and fixing sheets, as once the sheets are fixed, trolleys have to be moved, creating another gap in which to lay the next sheet. In addition, on long roofs the trolleys have to be linked and can create a gap for the whole length of the leading edge, which is undesirable.

224 In most situations, additional measures (usually in the form of fall arrest such as safety nets or harness and running line systems) are required to protect workers using trolley systems from falling through the gap created to lay a new sheet or through fragile material such as partially fixed liner sheets. Follow the manufacturer's recommendations on suitable anchorage points for running line systems. Horizontal guard rails on purlin trolleys or stagings are unlikely to be strong enough.

225 Trolley systems rely on the alignment of the supporting steelwork and the quality of the joints between purlins for the trolleys to run freely. Attempting to free trolleys that have jammed can be dangerous. They are not suitable where design details such as hips, dormers etc do not allow adequate support over the full length of the trolley.

226 For many reasons, trolley systems are often not practicable and should only be used where there is no safer alternative. However, where trolleys are used:

- there should be a safe system for installing and/or assembling them on the roof specified in the method statement;
- the trolley attachment/locking system should be suitable for the purlin design;
- a safe system for moving trolleys should be established;
- the joints between the purlins must allow the trolley to slide freely. Even minor misalignment can cause the trolley to jam and lead to unsafe systems of work;
- there should be a safe means of access to the trolley;
- when used as edge protection, the trolley must **always** be locked in position; and
- if there is risk of falling from the end of the trolley, eg at an unprotected ridge, a suitable barrier should be provided.

227 As the material loads get heavier due to increasing thickness and length, more people are required to manhandle the units. This will lead to other issues:

- failing to all lift together could result in sprains;
- too many operatives plus their load concentrated on a small area of the roof may make a non-fragile-designed roof fragile;
- unco-ordinated moves between operatives can lead to an operative caught off-balance, leading to trips and falls; and
- handling roof panels of this size in anything other than calm weather will lead to serious manhandling problems.

Protecting the public

Figure 38(a) Tunnel

Figure 38(b) Debris netting (Image courtesy of Combisafe)

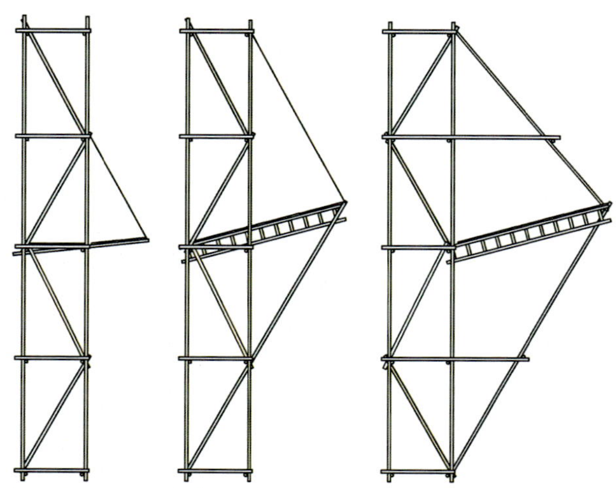

Figure 38(c) Scaffold fan classifications (Permission to reproduce extracts is granted by BSI)

228 The public may be at risk from falling materials or tools during roof work. Always take precautions to prevent materials falling where they may cause danger to anyone. This is particularly important where members of the public pass close to or below roof work. Where work has to be done and danger still exists, you may need to consider a pavement closure or diversion to make sure that the public are not put at risk for the duration of the work.

229 Birdcage scaffolds and debris netting can both be used to retain falling materials. Whatever system you chose, it should be capable of retaining whatever is likely to fall. If material is stacked on a scaffold platform above the height of the toe board, proprietary brick guards will be needed to prevent material falling onto other workers or the public below.

230 Where the public pass below or near to the scaffold, then scaffold fans, tunnels or similar arrangements may be required. Figures 38(a)–(c) show examples of debris netting, scaffold fans and tunnels.

231 Where a bitumen boiler is sited at ground level, a suitable exclusion zone will be required so that the public cannot access the boiler area. This is particularly important when a school or other similar public building is being refurbished. Physical barriers – not bunting – and an attendant are advisable.

A child walking down a pavement sustained head injuries when struck by a hammer dropped by a roof worker working on a residential property. A scaffold had been provided, but the edge protection was not adequate to contain falling materials.

A member of the public suffered serious head injuries when he was struck by a falling slate. A terraced house was being re-roofed. No edge protection was provided, and no precautions taken to prevent materials falling into the street.

232 Material may also fall through gaps in the working platform or between the working platform and the building. Sheeting, combined with a second layer of scaffold boards or plywood sheets, can be used to prevent this (see Figure 39). Take care not to overload the scaffold. If there is any risk of drips of hot bitumen falling from the roof edge, then physical protection or barriers at ground level may be necessary. See also Appendix 6.

233 Special precautions will be necessary where children may be put at risk (eg at or near schools or play areas or to keep them off scaffolding etc). It is advisable for the company carrying out the work to contact the head teacher of the school to make them directly aware of the work and its location. Where possible, roof work at schools should be done in holidays.

234 Never throw waste materials (such as old slates, tiles etc) from the roof or scaffold. It should be lowered in skips or baskets designed for the purpose, which will not spill material if snagged. Alternatively, enclosed debris chutes can be used (see Figure 7). Chutes should be closed off to prevent their use when the skip below has been removed. Skips should be covered where necessary to protect the public from dust and flying materials.

235 Do not hoist materials over the public. Either:

- find an alternative place for hoisting, eg at the rear of the premises; or
- use an alternative means of raising materials; or
- choose a time when the footpath can be closed (by agreement with the local highways authority).

236 Further advice on protecting the public from the hazards of construction work is given in *Protecting the public: Your next move* HSG151.

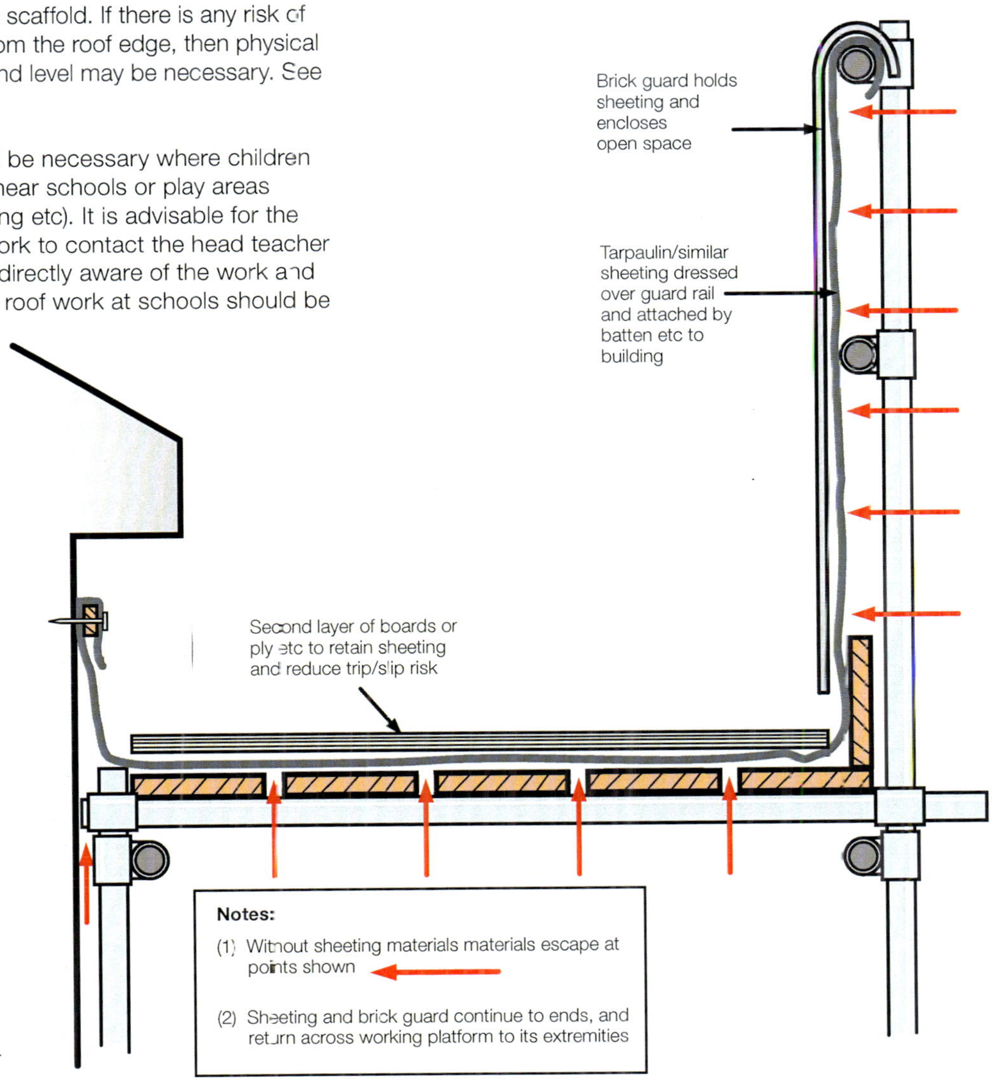

Figure 39 Suitable protection for use where the public could be at risk from falling objects or materials

Dealing with health risks

237 Falls and other safety issues are not the only risks linked to roof work. There are some significant health risks as well. The key ones are:

- manual handling;
- harmful dusts and chemicals; and
- vibration, noise and sun exposure.

238 Every year far more people are off work due to ill health caused in the workplace than as a result of any safety-related accident. Health risks need to be managed **at least** as well as safety risks. Do not wait for health problems to occur before putting in place control measures.

239 The main health risks that you need to be aware of are detailed below. For more information on these and other health risks go to: www.hse.gov.uk/construction/healthtopics/index.htm

Manual handling

240 Manual handling covers a wide variety of tasks including lifting, lowering, pushing, pulling and carrying. Common roof work tasks involve:

- loading out roof tiles;
- carrying mortar to roof level; and
- laying large roofing sheets.

241 If any of these tasks are not done properly there is a risk of accidents, injury and effects on health. This includes work-related musculoskeletal disorders (MSDs) such as back pain, upper and lower limb pain, and repetitive strain injuries of various sorts. Manual handling is one of the most common causes of ill health at work. Construction workers are particularly at risk and are off work due to back problems more than any other type of ill-health issue.

242 To help prevent MSDs try to avoid manual handling as far as possible. Ask 'Does the load need to be handled manually at all?', or 'Can the work be done in a different way?' For example, can materials be delivered directly to where they are going to be used instead of being manually carried, pushed or pulled?

243 If manual handling cannot be avoided then think about whether the work can be automated, mechanised (see Figure 40(a)–(c)), or if lifting equipment such as a gin wheel, gantry hoist or scaffold hoist can be used. Remember, the introduction of some solutions may introduce other risks that you will need to take into consideration.

Figure 40(a) Mechanical handling of large roof sheets (Images courtesy of Advisory Committee on Roofsafety), see also Figures 5(a) and 5(b)

Handling roof cladding

244 Before work starts, designers and specifiers should consider reducing the length of roof sheets. This makes the sheets lighter and reduces their unwieldy nature, particularly against weather conditions when handled at height. These advantages should be considered alongside the need to minimise work on the roof during installation, maintenance and repair.

245 Alternatively, designers can specify oversized roof sheets and gutters so that it is not possible to handle them manually and they have to be mechanically handled. Mechanical handling is always preferable where it is possible, see Figure 5(a).

Figure 40(b)

Figure 40(c)

246 Guidance on materials handling and storage for roof work involving steel frame buildings has been produced by the Steel Construction Institute.[22] It advises deliveries to be planned so that there is only the minimum need for storage on site without stopping progress of the work.

247 However, there will still be some need to store materials on site. Where needed, the storage location should be:

- decided before delivery;
- as close as possible to where the materials need to be used;
- easily accessible; and
- away from any access roads.

248 Wherever possible, materials should be offloaded directly from the delivery vehicle onto the roof. This avoids double handling of roof cladding packs and other materials.

249 When choosing where to store materials on the roof or scaffold, think carefully about where the load should go. Aim to minimise the need for further movement, but make sure the load does not damage the supporting structure or compromise others' safety.

Handling composite roof panels

250 Thicker and heavier composite roofing panels are now being used because of the laying of deeper insulation materials. These panels may be up to 30 m long and can weigh in excess of 250 kg. Installing these panels manually is dangerous and should not be undertaken. Handling teams are not appropriate as co-ordinating the workers is difficult. Manually lifting such a load can lead to one or more members of the team handling far more of the weight than others, increasing the risk of injury and also leading to additional risks such as slips, trips and falls.

251 Many types of mechanical handling equipment are available to avoid the need for manual lifting. Cranes, including mobile, telescopic and tower cranes, and self-erecting, trailer-mounted versions, are widely available for hire or purchase.

252 Figures 41(a)–(c) show a mechanical means of lifting and positioning long roof sheets. This significantly reduces the amount of manual handling needed. Long sheets are delivered interleaved with alternate ones turned over before hoisting to roof level. A vacuum device is used to lift the sheets by crane. There are also types of large 'bags' which can be used to hoist large, heavy, flat materials.

Other roof installation work

253 As well as work on the roof structure and coverings, many other tasks are carried out on roofs. This includes more recent developments such as fitting wind turbines and solar panels to domestic properties. Ways to mechanically lift such items onto the roof needs careful thought before the work is started.

Harmful dusts and chemicals

254 Roof work can involve exposure to many different dangerous dusts and chemicals, which might be harmful on contact or give off toxic fumes and vapours. The use of and generation of such hazardous substances should

Figure 41 24 m long roof panels being mechanically lifted from ground level and installed on roof (a) (b) (c)

always be avoided where possible. Where this is not possible, use the least hazardous product available that will perform satisfactorily and control the work to minimise the exposure to any harmful substances. Sometimes exposures cannot be avoided. Choosing the safest method of work, considering the method of application, is very important in these situations to protect people. Remember also to use PPE such as masks and gloves, where appropriate, as a final barrier.

Asbestos

255 Asbestos is the single biggest cause of work-related deaths in the UK. Asbestos-related diseases currently kill around 4000 people a year in Britain. However, as long as asbestos is in good condition and is not disturbed or damaged there is negligible risk. When disturbed or damaged, it can become a danger to health because asbestos fibres are released into the air and people can breathe them in. Although it is now illegal to use asbestos in the construction or refurbishment of any premises, many thousands of tonnes of it were used in the past in such things as insulation products for fireproof panels and in asbestos cement roofing material. Much of this material may still be in place. However, buildings built after 2000 are unlikely to contain asbestos-containing materials (ACM).

Identifying asbestos

256 Everyone involved in roof work needs to be aware of ACMs, including clients, designers and contractors. Any asbestos in the proposed work area needs to be identified before work is commissioned and starts. This includes:

- the amount;
- where it is and what condition it is in;
- whether work is likely to disturb the material; and, if so
- how the material needs to be safely protected or removed.

257 For demolition and refurbishment work it is essential to get information from existing records (such as the client's survey, asbestos plan or register) and by commissioning a suitable survey before any construction work starts. The need to survey for asbestos and protect or remove it should be included in the initial project cost and programme.

Asbestos training

258 Anyone who works with or is likely to come across ACMs needs to be aware of the risks. The minimum requirement is an asbestos awareness training course. This needs to cover the following topics:

- the properties of asbestos and its effects on health, including the increased risk of lung cancer for asbestos workers who smoke;
- the types, uses and likely occurrence of asbestos and ACMs in buildings and plant;
- the general procedures to be followed to deal with an emergency, eg an uncontrolled release of asbestos dust into the workplace; and
- how to avoid the risks of asbestos, eg no employee should carry out building work that disturbs the fabric of a building unless the employer has confirmed that ACMs are not present.

Common asbestos products

259 Roof workers may come into contact with or disturb a number of materials containing asbestos. The more common ones include:

- asbestos cement profiled sheets, flat sheets and slates;
- asbestos cement guttering and rainwater pipes;
- asbestos cement flue pipes passing through the roof;
- textured decorative coatings;
- asbestos-based felts and asbestos backing on metal sheets; and
- other products, such as floor tiles, mastics, sealants, rope seals and gaskets (in pipework etc), millboard, paper products, cloth (fire blankets etc) and bitumenous products (roofing felt etc).

260 In general, work can be done on these products so long as workers have had training that includes safe work practices, control measures and protective equipment for working with these ACMs, and that the risk assessment for the work shows the concentration of asbestos fibres in the air will not exceed exposure limits.

261 There are some instances where this work is best avoided if possible. For example, cleaning an asbestos cement roof can release asbestos fibres. High-pressure water jets should not be used, as the contaminated slurry is difficult to contain.

Licensed asbestos work

262 There is a very high risk of asbestos fibre release when working on some roof materials. In particular, these include:

- insulation board, eg in soffits and roof linings;
- sprayed asbestos, eg on structural roof members and applied as a coating to asbestos cement sheets; and
- asbestos pipe insulation, eg in roof spaces.

263 Work involving these products is high risk. The law requires it to be undertaken only by contractors with specialist knowledge, equipment and training who are licensed by HSE.

264 The HSE website (www.hse.gov.uk/asbestos/index.htm) provides further information, including advice on:

- how to carry out work with asbestos-containing materials;
- the type of controls necessary;
- what training is required; and
- what work must be carried out by licensed contractors.

Lead

265 Lead remains a versatile and widely used material in roof work. It is used for flashing, rainwater goods and making difficult junctions watertight, as well as a roof covering in some instances. It is also a hazardous substance which is harmful to health when inhaled or ingested and can cause severe short-term and long-term health problems. Roof workers can be exposed to lead when:

- carrying out hot work, cutting or joining lead materials; and
- removing or repairing old lead roofs.

266 Any risks from lead need to be taken into account before starting work. Alternatives should be used where possible such as glass-reinforced plastic (GRP), PVC, felt and plastics. Steps to control exposure need to be put in place where lead is used. These include:

- good welfare, including hot water, soap and towel for washing hands and face, a place to eat and drink away from the work area;
- work methods that reduce the risk of exposure to lead fume and dust; and
- instruction and training for workers so that they understand the risks and the purpose of the control measures.

267 Lead can also present a manual handling problem due to its weight. Again, you can reduce this risk by using lighter alternatives such as GRP, PVC, felt or plastics. However, where lead is required, mechanical lifting devices (such as hoists, cranes or gin wheels) should be used to eliminate or reduce the need to manually handle rolls of lead.

A client wanted the designer to produce a design with ornamental roof features. The initial intention was to produce the features from cast iron, lead and copper, which would have required risky manual handling to lift them into position and fit them. Redesigning the features slightly allowed them to be produced as a single, lightweight GRP moulding, which could be easily lifted and bolted into place. The reduction in weight substantially reduced the potential for serious manual handling safety.

Silica

268 Silica is found in many types of stone and in concrete, including roof tiles. In dust form it will be released during cutting or grinding. Inhaling silica dust can lead to serious disease, including lung cancer and more than 500 workers die each year from silica-related diseases.

269 Even short periods of roof tile cutting can create high levels of silica dust. Where possible, cutting should be eliminated by using ½ or 1½ size tiles. Where resizing is needed, use water to stop the dust getting into the air. Modern cut-off saws have an attachment for a water hose.

270 Cutting should not be undertaken on the roof but on an area of the surrounding scaffolding set up for this purpose. Where practical this also applies to valleys. For example, GRP valley systems with a central 'ridge' enable valley tiles to be first marked against this ridge and then taken down onto the scaffolding for cutting.

271 When using such a cutting area it is vital that the safety of the scaffold boards is not affected. A suitable piece of sacrificial material should be placed between the tile and scaffold boards to prevent the boards being accidentally cut. The water jets of the cut-off saw and water container need to be inspected and maintained regularly to keep them in working order.

272 Even with water suppression some silica dust will still remain in the air and a mask should also be worn. Nuisance-grade dust masks do not protect the lungs. Use either a FFP3 disposable mask or a half mask with P3 filters. Wearers must be face fit tested to make sure the mask works correctly.

Bitumen and asphalt

273 Bitumen comes from natural heavy crude oil deposits or from petroleum refining. It is commonly used as an adhesive to bond reinforced bitumen membranes (RBM) onto the deck or insulation board. The term is often interchanged with 'asphalt'.

274 Hot bitumen can create a number of health issues. These include:

- throat and eye irritation from the vapours;
- skin irritation/dermatitis; and
- burns.

275 These health issues can occur, in particular, where:

- natural ventilation is poor, eg by adjacent structures or when near to bitumen boilers;
- hot bitumen could get onto the skin when being used; suitable gloves and overalls need to be worn; or
- larger quantities of hot bitumen are being moved, particularly from the ground to the roof.

Glues and solvents

276 There are a variety of roofing products that use or contain glues and solvents. They can present risks through:

- breathing in vapours;
- contact with the skin or eyes; or
- eating and drinking food with contaminated hands.

277 The main effects are irritation of the skin, eyes and lungs, headache, nausea, dizziness and light-headedness. Exposure can damage co-ordination and increase the likelihood of accidents such as falling off ladders. Concentration on important/difficult tasks can also be lost and those affected may react more slowly to dangerous situations. Very high exposures can cause unconsciousness and even death, for instance where adhesives are used in unventilated confined spaces or where there is significant spillage.

278 The type of glues and solvents used will have a very big impact on the potential dangers. Because of this, designers should first consider whether a less harmful substance could be used. When selecting a glue or solvent it is important to find out about the risks linked to it. The information on the package label and the safety data sheet provided by the manufacturer should provide help on the control measures needed.

279 Possible control measures include:

- brush application rather than spraying;
- ventilation to dilute or extract the fumes;
- wearing a suitable and properly fitted mask;
- suitable gloves to prevent skin contact; and
- adequate washing facilities.

280 Sufficient instruction and training will be needed to make sure that the risks and precautions are understood.

Biological hazards

281 Not all hazardous substances are generated by work activities. Animal waste, decaying litter or pests may be found when entering roof spaces and can cause ill health in roofers. Breathing in dust from dried bird droppings can cause psitticosis and contact through broken skin with rat urine can lead to Weil's disease (leptospirosis).

282 Droppings should not be removed by using high pressure water. This can cause dust from the droppings to get into the air where it could be breathed in. However, generally wetting down the work area is advised. Containing the work area with plastic sheeting should also be considered. If appropriate, a P3 or FFP3 mask should be used. Overalls should be worn, and replaced when they are soiled. Workers who may be susceptible to an infection should not be directly involved in the removal of droppings.

283 Leptospirosis enters through skin cuts and abrasions or through the mucous membrane lining of the nose, mouth and conjunctiva (eye). The organism may also be ingested via food or water contaminated by rat urine.

284 High standards of personal hygiene by provision and use of adequate welfare facilities are essential for controlling these risks.

Welfare for all construction sites

285 Good welfare facilities should always be provided. They are the basis for controlling exposure to many common harmful substances. Basic requirements are:

- a supply of hot and cold water and soap for washing;
- bowls/sinks big enough to allow hands and forearms to be washed easily before eating or drinking; and
- clean towels.

286 Washing facilities should include the provision of showers if required by the nature of the work or for health reasons.

Vibration and noise

Vibration

287 Workers may be exposed to hand-arm vibration (HAV) when operating hand-held power tools such as cut-off saws or hammer drills. Regular and frequent exposure to HAV can lead to permanent ill health. Damage may occur to blood vessels, nerves and musculoskeletal structures. HAV can cause a range of painful and distressing symptoms including hand-arm vibration syndrome (HAVS) and carpal tunnel syndrome.

288 Where workers are exposed to HAV dangers the extent of that exposure should be assessed and eliminated, or reduced to as low a level as reasonably practicable.

289 Risk control should follow the hierarchy of using other work methods or equipment to prevent vibration exposure where possible. Otherwise, equipment should be chosen with the least vibration exposure, ensuring it is maintained and parts replaced as appropriate, with exposure times limited through work scheduling and rotations of tasks. Users of vibrating tools should be trained in the risks and how to minimise their exposure, and health surveillance provided where appropriate.

Sources of vibration information

290 Information on the levels of vibration from the tools used should reflect normal use (ie equipment in use at work.) Further guidance can be found at: www.hse.gov.uk/construction/healthtopics/vibration.htm.

Noise

291 Frequent exposure to high noise levels causes irreversible damage to hearing, which may be accompanied by tinnitus (a sensation of noises or ringing in the ears). The longer the exposure and the higher the noise level, the quicker this damage will become noticeable.

292 Exposure to noise from work activities should be assessed and controlled. Once risks to hearing have been controlled to the lowest level practicable, hearing protection should be provided if risks remain.

293 Noise on construction sites usually comes from machinery and tools used for demolition, excavation or piling and from compressors and concrete mixers etc. Other operations, such as hammering, riveting and the use of cartridge-operated fixing tools, may also be a source of excessive noise. It is important to note that workers may be exposed to noise generated from other workers on a site – not just the noise that they themselves produce.

294 Manufacturers and suppliers of equipment have to provide information on the noise their equipment produces. Although loud noise is obvious, if someone has to shout to be heard at two metres away for part of the day then there is likely to be damaging noise exposures.

Control

295 Can the job be done in another way that does not involve using noisy equipment? If not, can quieter equipment be used that will get the job done in the most efficient way? Poor maintenance of tools can also lead to increased noise levels. Carrying out a noisy job well away from where other people are working will also help, as will moving workers out of the immediate vicinity and putting up signs to keep people out. Health surveillance should also be given to workers where there remains a risk to their health.

296 Noise levels can be reduced by making sure the exhausts of compressors, generators and other plant are directed away from work areas. Screens faced with sound absorbent materials can be placed around plant.

297 If it is not possible to eliminate the noise source or reduce the noise, provide workers with ear defenders (muffs or plugs). But remember that providing hearing protection is not a substitute for noise elimination and control at source.

298 Further guidance can be found at: www.hse.gov.uk/construction/healthtopics/noise.htm.

Sun exposure

299 Roof workers will be significantly exposed to sunlight. They are therefore at particular risk from heat exhaustion and the effects of ultraviolet radiation on the skin. Cancer of the skin is the commonest form of cancer. Simple precautions can significantly reduce the risk of skin cancer and heat exhaustion, eg:

- wearing suitable clothing, such as long sleeve and trousers made from high wicking material with UV protection;
- use of sun screens of at least protection factor 30;
- suitable rest periods or rotating work to avoid lengthy exposures during the middle of the day and
- regularly drinking water.

Training and competence for roof workers

300 Roof work is potentially dangerous and roof workers need appropriate knowledge, skills and experience to carry out roof work safely and competently. A competent roofer will be one who has:

- sufficient knowledge of the specific task to be undertaken and the risks the work will entail; and
- sufficient experience and ability to carry out their duties in relation to the work, to recognise their limitations and take appropriate action to prevent harm to those carrying out the roof work or those affected by the work.

301 Trainees or less experienced roof workers need to be under the supervision of a competent person.

302 If you control the work of roof workers operating at height, you should have clear procedures that identify those tasks or work activities which require specific competences, and authorise only competent workers to carry them out.

303 Developing competence in health and safety is an ongoing process. Individuals will develop their competence through experience in the job and through training, which is part of 'lifelong learning'.

304 Passing the basic Construction Skills Health and Safety Test, or an equivalent, provides evidence of a threshold of health and safety knowledge appropriate for a new starter in construction.

305 To achieve competence, workers should be trained in safe working practices and those health and safety issues specific to their trade. It is not enough to hope that they will 'pick up' safety on the job from other workers – they might simply be learning someone else's bad habits. Employers need to be sure of their employees' abilities before setting them to work and should provide training where it is required. Roof workers will need training on the risks they will encounter (such as recognising fragile materials) and safe systems of work to control them.

306 British Standard BS 8454:2006[23] provides guidance and recommendations on the delivery of training and education for work at height, including rescue.

307 Appropriate Construction Scottish Vocational Qualifications or Qualification and Credit Framework (QCF) qualifications with NVQ in the title at Level 2 or 3 is the best available evidence that an individual roof worker has achieved an appropriate level of competence. Scottish Vocational Qualifications or QCF NVQs can be attained in a range of specific roofing trades and occupations.

308 Training provided for roof workers should make sure that trainees gain an awareness of the following elements of health and safety knowledge:

- main provisions of the Work at Height Regulations 2005;
- the work at height hierarchy;
- interpreting risk assessments and method statements;
- fragile surfaces;
- edge protection;
- access and egress, eg stair towers and ladders;
- nets;
- manual handling;
- selection and type of work equipment, eg hoists;
- workplace inspections;
- scaffold awareness;
- harness training and inspection;
- rescue training;
- plant, ie MEWPs;
- environment, ie weather conditions;
- fitness to work; and
- tools and equipment.

309 Further specialist training will be required for specific types of roof work or for tasks such as tower scaffold erection, operating a MEWP, emergency rescue, net rigging etc.

310 Other workers also have to access roofs, eg safety advisors, engineers, designers, quantity surveyors, maintenance staff, and plant installers to name but a few. They will also need training in working at height (that reflects the activities they are expected to carry out) before they can be deemed competent to work on a roof.

311 Managers and supervisors need to be competent to deliver safety standards on site. To achieve this they will need health and safety training to:

- assess and prioritise the risks on a particular project;
- design safe systems of work that are appropriate to specific site conditions; and
- prepare clear, simple safety method statements that can be used and understood by site workers.

312 First-line supervisors need to be able to interpret a safety method statement and explain and follow a safe system of work.

313 Managers and supervisors who control roof work require specific training. For example, the Construction Skills 'Site Management Safety Training Scheme' five-day course for site managers, or the two-day 'Site Supervisors' Safety Training Scheme', or equivalent courses.

314 Everyone who uses personal protective equipment should know how to use it effectively, eg:

- how to inspect the equipment to make sure that it will operate satisfactorily (see *Inspecting fall arrest equipment made from webbing or rope* INDG367[24]);
- how to fit and use a safety harness, following the manufacturer's recommendations; and
- how to check the face fit of a respirator or dust mask.

315 Every contractor carrying out roof work needs to make sure that a named individual is responsible for the health and safety functions. The named individual may need extra training in health and safety to meet their responsibilities properly. Contractors also need to have access to competent advice.

Construction (Design and Management) Regulations 2007

316 This section describes what clients, co-ordinators, principal contractors and contractors need to do to comply with the Construction (Design and Management) Regulations 2007 (CDM).

The role of the client

317 Those who own, occupy or have responsibility for a building have an important role to play when arranging for roof work to be done. This includes considering the design and specification of a new building, appointing a contractor for refurbishment, or organising for an emergency repair.

318 CDM applies to all construction projects, with the exception of domestic clients. If you appoint someone for a project, you should take reasonable steps to make sure that they are competent for the job they are to do.

319 Assessment of competence is a two-stage process:

Stage 1: Assess the company's organisation and arrangements for health and safety to determine whether they enable them to do the work safely and without risk.

Stage 2: Assess the company's experience and track record to establish that it is capable of doing the work safely.

A set of core criteria for assessing competence are given in Appendix 4 of *Managing health and safety in construction* L144. Stage 1 and 2 assessments should be made against these criteria.

320 The client should make sure that relevant pre-construction information is provided to those who need it, so that work can be carried out safely. This could include information on:

- what an existing roof is made of;
- the age of an existing roof;
- previous modifications to an existing roof;
- existing arrangements for access to the roof;
- restrictions on availability of space for cranes;
- any relevant permit-to-work arrangements operated by the client;
- fire precautions on an occupied site; and
- areas where contractor access is prohibited.

321 Where a project is notifiable (ie where the client is not a domestic client, and the construction phase will last more than 30 days or more than 500 person days), the client must appoint a CDM co-ordinator and a principal contractor. The co-ordinator should act as the client's key advisor for health and safety matters so it is important that the co-ordinator be appointed as soon as possible.

322 There are no duties placed on domestic clients. However, other clients should take reasonable steps to make sure that the contractor's arrangements for managing the project allow the work to be carried out without risks to health and safety. (If the project is notifiable this will include a construction phase plan by the principal contractor.) There should also be suitable arrangements for the welfare of construction workers (toilet, washing and rest facilities).

323 If clients dictate the design details (eg that specific materials will be used) then the client should comply with the duties placed on designers by CDM (see paragraphs 326–349).

324 Unrealistic building or refurbishment programmes can lead to undue pressure on those carrying out the work. This can make it harder for contractors to plan for safe working, to prepare quality safety method statements and to review and amend systems of work. Clients have an important role here – they must not place unreasonable demands on the project.

325 Under CDM, clients have a role to play in construction work including roof work. They must:

- provide enough time and resource to allow the project to be delivered safely;
- take reasonable steps to make sure that management arrangements, including their own, are suitable so that construction work can be carried out without risk to health and safety so far as is reasonably practicable;
- make sure that welfare facilities are provided on the site;
- the structure that has been designed complies with the Workplace (Health, Safety and Welfare) Regulations 1992;[25]
- provide pre-construction information about the project to interested parties. This should be project-specific health and safety information and be provided to designers and contractors at an early stage;
- check the competence of those whom they appoint;
- co-operate; and
- co-ordinate their activities.

The role of the designer

326 Using their professional skills and judgement, designers can eliminate hazards at source and make risks easier to manage. This helps contractors to provide a safer place of work on the roof. Designers need to consider initial construction work as well as future maintenance, cleaning, proposed use and demolition requirements.

327 Under CDM, designers have a duty to eliminate hazards that may give rise to risks, and to reduce the risks from any remaining hazards so far as is reasonably practicable. They should also:

- make sure clients are aware of their duties;
- make sure that they (the designer) are competent;
- co-ordinate their work with others as necessary to manage risk;
- co-operate with the CDM co-ordinator and others; and
- provide information for the health and safety file.

328 Designers have to avoid foreseeable risks, so far as is reasonably practicable, by:

- eliminating hazards from the construction, cleaning, maintenance, proposed use (workplace only) and demolition of any structure;
- reducing risks from any remaining hazard; and
- giving priority to design solutions that provide collective protection for all, rather than individual protection.

329 For example, they could:

- eliminate unprotected fragile materials;
- eliminate or, where this is not possible, minimise the need for work at height during construction;
- eliminate or minimise inspection and maintenance requirements for the completed roof structure;
- identify and design-in safe access and a safe place of work for maintenance and cleaning (see Figure 42);
- carefully consider where to site plant that will need maintenance. Are there alternatives to placing it on the roof? If not, is it in the best position on the roof for providing safe access?
- carefully consider the siting of roof lights and how they will be protected should access be necessary in the future (see Figure 43);
- provide clear and unambiguous specifications for safety-critical elements of the design; and
- provide information relevant to construction and maintenance for inclusion in pre-construction information, tender documentation and in the health and safety file.

Figure 42 Permanent walkway giving safe access on a fragile roof. (This walkway was retrofitted, but similar access can be included in initial designs)

Figure 43 Lighting panels installed in the wall rather than the roof

Example of risk elimination through design

On the major refurbishment of a large hangar, the fragile asbestos cement roof was replaced by load-bearing metal sheets. After consultation with the client, the roof lights were replaced by translucent vertical panels below eaves level. This reduced risk of falls during re-roofing and any subsequent maintenance (see Figure 43).

Examples of reduction/control of risk through design

The designer of a new shopping centre with a glass atrium recognised the risk of falling during cleaning and maintenance of glazed areas. An access system using mobile gantries was designed and installed and an inspection regime established for the equipment.

The designer of a 'built-up' industrial roof made sure that all components, eg liner panels, top sheets, insulation and fixings, were the same modular width. This reduced the risk to roof workers. They were able to adopt a system of work that restricted the area of temporarily fixed liner panels to a single sheet width.

330 Outcomes such as those in the examples above are easier to achieve if there is good liaison between:

- designer and client, eg on access requirements for maintenance; and
- lead designer, contractors, specifiers and installers.

331 The designer should make sure that the client is aware of their duties under CDM. Where the project is notifiable, the designer can only do initial design work until a CDM co-ordinator has been appointed.

332 Paragraphs 333–346 provide more detailed design guidance for particular roofing applications.

Designing flat and low-pitch roofs

333 Access to these roofs is often simple and because they are flat it is easy to walk around on them. Accidents happen not just to roof workers but also to engineers, surveyors, children, caretakers etc. The first priority is to design-out the risk at source, eg by specifying adequate built-in edge protection. Designers should consider the alternatives available in terms of their effectiveness in preventing falls, as well as cost, aesthetics and ease of build.

Edge protection

334 Edge protection options in order of effectiveness are:

- designed parapet (see Figure 44);
- guard rail at the roof edge (see Figure 45);
- permanent protected walkway for access to plant on the roof;
- preformed sockets to support temporary edge protection guard rails;
- running line (rigid and flexible-line horizontal restraint/ fall-arrest systems) systems designed, installed and tested to the relevant standards (see Appendix 3).

Figure 44 Parapet edge protection included as an integral design feature

Figure 45 Permanent guard rail retrofitted during refurbishment work. Similar protection can be included in initial designs (Image courtesy of Safesite Limited)

335 Designers should take account of the provisions of the Workplace (Health, Safety and Welfare) Regulations 1992 if designing any structure that is to be used as a workplace.

Designing industrial roofs

336 The most important issue for designers is how to eliminate unprotected fragile material at height. **Designers should carefully consider the potential to eliminate or reduce this hazard.**

337 Whatever roof light and roofing sheet systems are used, the assembly should be tested to determine fragility and the relevant information passed on to those who may need it (see Appendix 4).

338 The health and safety file should include relevant information from the supplier, such as:

- test results on the initial material strength;
- the effects of ultraviolet radiation on material properties; and
- fixing specifications, including type, number and position.

Roof lights

339 **For roof lights designers should carefully consider the potential to eliminate or reduce this hazard.** The decision on whether to include roof lights should take account of the risks associated with temporary gaps during construction, and the risks when access to the roof is needed later, eg during inspection, maintenance or cleaning.

340 Where roof lights **are** required designers should consider:

- specifying non-fragile roof lights;
- fitting roof lights designed to project above the plane of the roof and that cannot be walked on (these reduce the risk but they should still be capable of withstanding a person falling onto them) (see Figure 46);
- protecting roof lights, eg by means of mesh or grids fitted below the roof light or between the layers of a built-up roof light (see Figure 47); or
- specifying roof lights with a design life that matches that of the roof, taking account of the likely deterioration due to ultraviolet exposure, environmental pollution and internal and external building environments.

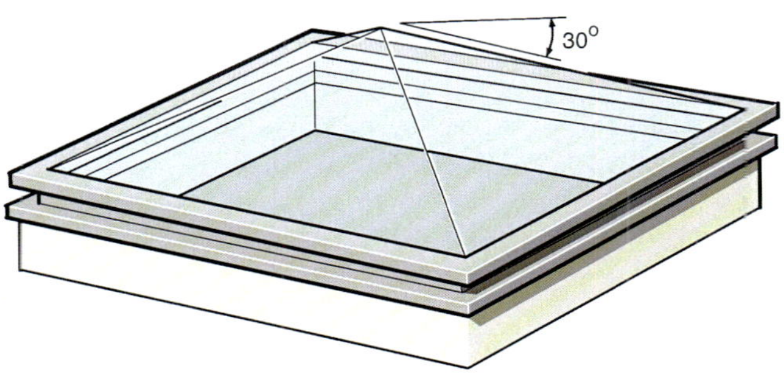

Figure 46 Typical 'out of plane' polycarbonate roof light

Figure 47 Galvanised mesh reinforcement between sheets of twin-skin roof light

341 Where existing fragile roof lights are present, covers can be retrofitted. See Figure 48.

Roofing sheets

342 The safest option for roof sheets is to specify a material that will be non-fragile for the design life of the roof. The norm should be to specify non-fragile roof sheets unless there are particular design requirements that dictate other materials. These design criteria should be clearly documented.

343 The specification of **reinforced** fibre cement sheets can be considered. These should still be considered fragile and appropriate precautions are needed when people work on or near them. However, they offer a less-fragile alternative to non-reinforced sheets.

344 There are usually times during the laying of a built-up roof when coverings are not load bearing, eg when not fully fixed. Designers need to consider this carefully and aim to eliminate or minimise this condition. The specification of liner sheets (thickness and profile) and, equally important, the fixing method should be assessed with these criteria in mind. The designer should supply precise information on the fixing configuration(s) that are load bearing for a particular span and cladding material combination (see Appendix 4) so that contractors can develop a safe system of work.

A roof worker was working over a temporarily fixed roof liner panel, putting in permanent fixings. He fell 10 m to his death when the end of the sheet buckled under his weight.

345 Composite roof sheets are quicker to fix and are often immediately load bearing independent of fixings. However, safe systems of work for handling these heavier sheets will need to be developed and the designer should consider this hazard and potential solutions (see paragraphs 240–253).

346 Handling very long roofing sheets can be dangerous for roof workers and others, even in moderate winds. Designers need to decide the maximum wind speed in which these sheets can be laid. They then need to find out about likely local weather conditions and this should indicate whether the proposed sheet lengths are appropriate or not. See advice on weather conditions given in paragraphs 63–74.

Figure 48 Covers can be fitted to existing roofs or included as part of the design (Image courtesy of Safesite Limited)

Roof maintenance

347 Designers can help to reduce the amount of work done at height throughout the life of the structure. For example, they could:

- increase the maintenance life of roof elements;
- locate plant and equipment at low level wherever possible; and
- design gutter detailing to reduce blockages.

Co-operating with others

348 Good liaison between designers can achieve better standards at all stages of the work. A practical example is the effect of gutter design on systems of work when the roof is laid. Roof workers and others commonly use gutters for access at eaves level along the roof. Gutters should only be used as access if the structural strength of the gutter and the quality of the fixings are suitable and sufficient. Areas used for access at height must be stable, strong enough and of sufficient dimensions to allow safe passage of people and any plant or materials they require and be fitted with handrails or other means to prevent falls. Problems can often be avoided if designers consult with each other and one takes into account means of access if it will be required for some users.

349 There are a number of issues where the design of the frame of the structure directly affects the roof workers' systems of work. For example:

- if running lines are to be used during erection, anchorage points need to be designed into the frame at appropriate points;
- the design and sizing of purlins and the alignment of the joints between purlins can determine whether or not a trolley system can be used successfully;
- the position of anti-sag rods can affect systems of work; and
- the design of eaves beams affects the installation of nets and the stability of scaffold-tube edge protection.

Resolving these issues requires close co-ordination between frame and cladding designers.

Designing trussed roofs

350 Designers of trussed roofs can contribute to safe working by:

- designing both permanent and temporary bracing so that it can be fixed from a safe place;
- designing slinging points and lifting attachments, which allow truss bundles to be unslung from a safe place, eg the eaves scaffold;
- designing permanent bracing to allow trusses to be pre-assembled into complete roof structures or modules on the ground and lifted into position;
- specifying slinging points for such assemblies; and
- giving information on the bracing required before a working platform can be supported by the trusses.

CDM co-ordinators

351 CDM co-ordinators have an important role to play where CDM applies. It is a proactive role and should not be seen as an auditing/checking role, eg:

- they must advise the client on competence when appointing designers and contractors;
- they will identify and collect the pre-construction information and advise the client of any gaps in the information which may require further surveys/investigations; and
- they will advise the client on the adequacy of the construction phase plan provided by the principal contractor.

352 The pre-construction information should cover:

- the major health and safety risks on the project;
- whether significant resources are needed to control these risks; and
- what specific competencies are required to carry out the work safely.

353 The pre-construction information should:

- set out any basic assumptions about how the work will be done to control any significant risks, eg using safety nets for industrial roofs, or using mobile access equipment to install gutters and erect edge protection;
- identify programming implications of safe systems of work, eg providing suitable ground conditions for mobile access equipment, allowing time for blockwork to cure before trusses are installed;
- identify any aspects of the clients' activities that have health and safety implications, eg times when significant vehicle movements can be expected; and
- clarify any other specific requirements by the client, eg for repairs to a school roof, the client might specify that work is done during school holidays.

For a new warehouse, the pre-construction information specified that a hardstanding concrete floor would be in place for the structural erection phase. This enabled roofing contractors to consider the use of MEWPs (either for the roofing work or to help install safety nets).

354 The pre-construction information should contain relevant information provided by the client or by designers, eg:

- the load-bearing capacity of a flat roof;
- ground conditions and access for crane(s);
- information from the designer on sequence of erection, temporary stability and bracing of trussed roofs;
- presence of asbestos insulation board in soffits;
- presence of sprayed asbestos on trusses or purlins;
- position and type of overhead power lines, including those associated with railways; and
- information on the design of fixing details necessary to ensure non-fragility.

Principal contractors

355 Principal contractors set the practical on-site safety standards and make sure that they are actually followed. They should:

- make sure that those they appoint are competent for the type of work;
- make sure that the overall work programme gives enough time for work to be done safely by the roofing subcontractor, taking account of likely weather conditions;
- allow time to consider method statements and liaise with the CDM co-ordinator on the implications of design changes;
- devise a work programme that reflects the need to control access to areas below roof work where there is danger of falling materials;
- clearly specify at the tender stage the resources allocated to control and manage risks such as falls from height; and
- make sure that relevant information is passed to the roofing contractor.

356 Principal contractors need to make sure that a suitable construction phase plan is in place before construction starts. The plan should state how health and safety will be managed during the construction phase, identify risks specific to the type of work, and include suitable and sufficient measures to address the risks, including any site rules. Any work at height is potentially high risk, so the plan should include enough detail for the risks to be controlled.

357 The principal contractor may require contractors to submit written safety method statements. The method statements can help the principal contractor assess the contractor's competence, and can help plan and co-ordinate work on site to minimise risks to health and safety for all site workers. Where written safety method statements are submitted, the principal contractor should have arrangements to review and approve them.

358 Principal contractors need to monitor contractors to make sure they comply with the construction phase health and safety plan and should take positive action to remedy matters if risk is not being effectively controlled.

Contractors and subcontractors

359 Contractors need to:

- implement a safe system of work. A site-specific safety method statement can help with this;
- make sure that they and their employees are competent to carry out their specific tasks safely, including supervision on site; and
- co-operate with the principal contractor, and help develop and implement the construction phase plan.

Appendix 1 Issues for method statements in industrial roof work

1 This appendix is not a method statement. It lists the issues that method statements need to cover for industrial roof work. A similar analytical approach is appropriate for other roof work.

2 Roof work is high risk and requires close attention to detail at all stages. There should be a job-specific method statement in writing, agreed and understood by all parties before work starts. Rigorous supervision is needed to make sure that the agreed method is followed in practice. There should also be a system to allow necessary changes to be made and confirmed.

3 Method statements should be clear, concise and include simple sketches where necessary.

4 Except for the simplest jobs, where the necessary precautions are straightforward and can be easily repeated (eg using a proper roofing ladder to replace a ridge tile), you should prepare safety method statements relating specifically to the job in hand. They should clearly describe the precautions and systems of work identified during the risk assessment. Everyone involved in the work needs to know what the method statement says and what they have to do – if they cannot understand the precautions or systems then they should not carry out the work. Make sure you have arrangements for supervision during the work to check that procedures are followed.

5 The method statement should cover the following areas:

- safe access;
- edge protection and other fall prevention such as working platforms;
- fall mitigation systems such as nets or air/bean bags;
- fragile materials;
- reducing the need for workers to move about the roof, eg by arranging for the right materials to be lifted to the right place at the right time;
- making sure that warning signs are displayed on existing roofs, particularly at roof access points; and
- supervision.

6 The following general questions are particularly relevant to low-pitch industrial roofs consisting of liner sheet, insulation layer and profiled metal top sheet. Non-standard or unusual systems will need further consideration. You may also need to address risks specific to an individual site (eg the presence of overhead power lines). This is not an exhaustive checklist, but is intended to act as a prompt when method statements are prepared and reviewed.

Table 10 Checklist for preparing method statements

Risk of falling, eg getting on/off ladders at eaves	Access to roof: ■ Have you discussed access points with the roofing team to reduce travel over the roof to a minimum? ■ If ladders are used (as opposed to tower scaffolds or stair towers, which are preferred), is equipment available for hoisting or craning components up? ■ Has the stability of long ladders been considered, eg will they need staying to reduce whip?
Risk of falling when walking past open edges to fetch materials	Materials handling: ■ How are roofing packs loaded out onto the roof? ■ Is this planned to reduce travel when fetching sheets and does it allow for protected routes/safe access? ■ Splitting packs of different sheet size and reassembling them at ground level can save travel at height. Back-loading sheets onto the completed roof can reduce travel past open edges.
Risk of falling from the building when unslinging	Cranes: ■ If one is used, who will accept the load or unsling it? ■ How will they be protected from falling? ■ Have you considered using mobile access equipment for this task?

Risk of falling outside the building frame exists at all stages of work. Gable ends are particularly hazardous	Edge protection: ■ Does the programme make sure that eaves, gable ends and other open edges are protected before work starts? Protection will also be required at ridges unless work progresses at the same rate on both roof slopes. ■ What are the access arrangements for workers installing edge protection?
Risk of falling on both sides of gutter, ie inside and outside the building frame	Gutter fixing: ■ How will workers be protected from falling? Peripheral edge protection erected for roof workers will not be sufficient at this phase. ■ Has the use of mobile access equipment been considered as a first priority? ■ If the use of a running line or harness and lanyard is specified, who will erect and test the line, and are workers properly trained and competent in their use?
Risk of falling from partly completed roof	Leading edge protection: ■ How will you protect the leading edge? Has the use of safety nets been considered in the light of legal duties and risk assessment for the total roofing operation? ■ Stagings used as working platforms should be stable and of adequate width with handrails/running lines specified to suit the working practices. ■ Work done kneeling or bending needs careful attention as the worker's centre of gravity can extend over the leading edge. ■ What method is specified for moving stagings? ■ Is the method of work to be adopted when laying the first sheet specified? Some architectural features, eg hip ends, will require the working methods to be modified. These should be fully described. ■ Has fixing ridge capping/flashing been included in the system of work? Is effective edge protection provided at the gable end of the ridge? Does the method statement make it clear at what stage of construction materials such as liner panels become load bearing? The number and type of fixings required should be stated. Until this is achieved, they must be treated as fragile materials, ie unable to sustain someone's weight, and protection should be provided as above. Have any fragile materials been specified by the designer? If so, the designer should review the decision as a matter of urgency in terms of duties under CDM. For refurbishment work on existing roofs, are there any fragile materials on the roof, eg roof lights? These will have to be protected. How will this be achieved? If covers are to be used, are they strong enough, taking account of the span required? How will they be fixed and what is the system for their removal? Zoning the roof into working and non-working areas can reduce the number of roof lights that need to be protected. Specify the system for marking out the zones and for doing the work. If barriers marking the edge of the zones are within 2 m of fragile material, then they should be a continuous physical barrier – painted lines and warning tape are not suitable. Zoning should take account of travel to the working area by the roof workers and the need for materials to be moved around the roof. The system should protect all roof lights within working zones and adjacent to access routes.
Systems control	**Communication:** What are the arrangements for communicating the method statement and agreeing it with the roofing team? **Supervision:** What are the arrangements for making sure that the work proceeds according to the method statement? **Modifications:** What are the arrangements for agreeing any modifications to the method statement and communicating them to the roofing gang? **Validation:** What are the arrangements for making sure that the company safety advisor or other nominated competent person has reviewed, and is satisfied with, the system of work proposed?

Appendix 2 Use of safety nets

1 Safety nets can be effectively employed to reduce the distance of potential falls and to minimise their effects. They offer collective, passive safety as they protect everyone working within their boundary without those workers having to act to be protected. They allow a broad range of activity to continue with minimum restriction.

2 Safety nets have high energy absorption, and offer a 'soft landing' that minimises injury. They should always be fitted as close as possible to the underside of the working platform to minimise the distance and consequences of a fall.

3 Lightweight, square mesh nets offer the flattest span (less than 10% sag). In most roof work it is possible to position such a net so that, even at the point of maximum sag, it is less than 2 m from the roof surface. In this position the net is an effective guard – this standard should be reached wherever possible. Riggers should always aim to rig safety nets as close as possible to the roof surface.

4 Safety nets overlaid with an appropriate fine-mesh debris cover can also protect those who have to work or pass below. Think about the type of materials likely to fall, eg fixings or tools, when choosing the overlay material. Safety nets also have the advantage that materials are contained by the net and do not bounce.

5 Safety nets can be used effectively:

- to minimise injury due to falls from leading edges, through liner panels or through temporarily fixed materials in new-build roofing;
- to guard roof lights and fragile roof materials during cleaning, maintenance and replacing the roof; and
- to minimise injury from falls during roof truss erection, eg when fitting diagonal bracing.

Relevant standards

6 Safety nets should be manufactured to the requirements of European Standard BS EN 1263-1.[26] They should be erected in accordance with BS EN 1263-2[27] and the guidance given in BS 8411.[28]

7 There are four types or systems of safety net. 'System S' nets (used in the horizontal plane) are the type normally used to protect roofers.

Design and technical details

8 When rigging safety nets it is important to maintain their energy-absorbing characteristics. Too many fixing points and the net will become more rigid and imposes larger loads on the user, the structure and the net itself. Too few fixing points and the net will sag and deflect too much under load. The manufacturer's recommendations and BS EN 1263-1 should be followed on the number and spacing of fixing points. Check that the supporting structure is capable of resisting the expected anchorage loads.

9 When using attachment devices, seek advice from the manufacturer and check the rigger is competent working with these devices.

10 Wherever possible, rig nets to prevent falls of 2 m or more. If they are to be used to arrest falls greater than 2 m, they should have:

- an area greater than 35 m^2;
- a minimum side length (width) greater than 5 m; and
- maximum support spacing 2.5 m.

Anchorage points

11 An individual anchor point capacity of 6 kN, applied at 45° to the horizontal, should be available with a combined capacity over an adjacent series of anchor points of 4 kN, 6 kN, 4 kN. In general, purlins, sheeting rails and tube and fitting handrails will not meet these requirements, although evidence to demonstrate otherwise from a competent person may be appropriate.

12 Adequate clearance must be allowed below the net for it to function properly and avoid the risk of the faller striking objects or the floor before being arrested. Limits are specified in BS EN 1263-2 and BS 8411. This is generally referred to as 'clearance distance'.

13 Installing safety nets in phases is not good practice and should only be done where there is no other alternative. Where it is done the safety net must extend beyond the leading edge of the work by at least 3 m to allow for the likely horizontal trajectory of anyone falling from that edge (see Table 11).

Table 11 Fall heights and catching widths

Fall height	Catching width
<1.0 m	>2.0 m
<3.0 m	>2.5 m
<6.0 m	>3.0 m

Erection

14 Safety nets can be connected to the structure by tie ropes, attachment devices (some of which may be rigged remotely from the ground) or specially designed attachment points on the structure.

15 The risk to riggers erecting, moving and dismantling nets should be assessed and a safe system of work established. At all times, the following hierarchy should be followed:

- install remotely without working at height;
- use mobile elevating work platforms (MEWPs);
- use ladders for short-duration work upon completion of a risk assessment;
- roped access techniques may be appropriate in some buildings. This is specialised work and should only be undertaken by those trained and competent to carry it out (see *Guidelines on the use of rope access methods for industrial purposes*[29]). **Never use mobile access towers (MATs).**

16 Workers who erect nets should be aware of the relevant standards, trained and competent to carry out the work safely.

Rescue

17 It is important to have a rescue plan in place before rigging nets. This plan must be workable, with necessary equipment available for use. In many situations, the rigging contractor is not on site when someone may need recovery. The responsibility for making sure a rescue can be carried out rests with the principle contractor (where CDM applies) or the person in control of the site.

18 Safety nets and attachment systems should be properly maintained by a competent person (usually employed by the rigger). Ideally there should be an audit trail from the manufacturer through to the last use. This information should be documented and be readily available for inspection.

Repairs

19 Safety nets should only be repaired by a competent person. It is best practice for this to be carried out away from site in a controlled environment, with each repair documented and information readily available for inspection. The use of tags or labels affixed to the repair will aid identification on site.

Appendix 3 Use of personal fall-protection systems

1 Personal fall-protection systems are placed at the lower end of the work at height hierarchy. Avoidance, fall prevention (eg guard rails, MEWPs, scaffolds etc), collective safeguards (eg air bags, bean bags etc) and work-restraint systems should be considered first. The two most common types of personal fall-protection systems used in roof work are work restraint and fall arrest. The most important points are summarised below.

2 For guidance on other types of personal fall protection (such as work positioning, rope access etc), you should seek the advice of individuals or companies who are trained and experienced in the use of such techniques.

Selecting precautions

3 When selecting the precautions to use to protect against falls from a roof you must follow the hierarchy of measures set out in paragraphs 16–17 of this book. When applying the hierarchy to a personal fall-protection system, consider the relevant features of work restraint and fall-arrest systems set out in Table 12.

Table 12 Features of work restraint and fall arrest

Work restraint	Fall arrest
Prevents falls	Minimises consequences of a fall
Provides personal protection – not collective	Provides personal protection – not collective
Is an active system – not passive	Is an active system – not passive

Training and supervision

4 A fall-protection system relies on the user's competence and discipline to make sure that the system is used consistently and effectively. Supervising people under your control is as important as training them.

5 Fall-protection systems are not foolproof and their safe use is not always common sense. Without proper training in fitting, use, maintenance, installation and equipment limitations, all that a fall-protection system can provide is a false sense of security.

6 Adequate information, instruction, training and supervision should be given when a fall-protection system is used, eg:

- how to select the correct products for the work situation;
- how to wear the harness and adjust it to the body;
- how to use and adjust the lanyard and other equipment;
- how to self-rescue or assist others after a fall;
- how to inspect the equipment and recognise significant defects;
- how to assemble the system correctly; and
- how to recognise and attach safely to approved anchorage points.

7 Initial training should be carried out by the supplier of the fall-protection system or by in-house trainers who have been trained and assessed by the system supplier. Trainees should be assessed for competence by carrying out typical tasks.

8 Refresher training should be carried out at appropriate intervals (normally three-yearly) followed by assessment of competence by again carrying out typical tasks at height.

9 Trainees should not be exposed to additional risk while carrying out tasks during training. Before beginning training, the training organisation should carry out a thorough risk assessment and put in place any necessary control measures, such as a back-up or secondary safety rope.

General considerations

10 All decisions regarding the use of fall protection equipment should be properly risk assessed and method statements, supervision and management controls should be employed during work.

11 There are a number of elements to a fall-protection system, typically an anchor point or anchor line, a connecting element such as an adjustable or fixed lanyard and a full body harness. Examples include:

- a single lanyard incorporating an energy absorbing element, a full body harness and an approved single anchor point;
- a horizontal anchor line with multiple anchors that can support a number of workers using full body harnesses and lanyards incorporating energy absorbing elements;

- a retractable-type fall arrester, a full body harness and an approved connector such as a sling, which could be tethered to structural steelwork that has been approved for attachment of the fall-arrest system.

12 Make sure that all of the elements are compatible with each other. You may need to check with manufacturers or suppliers as to the compatibility of the elements that make up your chosen system.

13 The size, weight and number of users should be taken into account when selecting the appropriate fall-protection system. Refer to the manufacturer's instructions for use for further guidance.

14 The elements that make up a fall-protection system should be tested and conform to the requirements of the relevant European standards and carry a CE mark, accompanied by the notified body's registration number.

15 The safe performance of a fall-protection system depends on connection to a suitable structural anchor. If a fall occurs and the structural anchor fails, then the fall-protection system will be of no benefit at all. The suitability of the anchor, and its supporting structure, to withstand the imposed loads and particularly any fall arrest loads without the risk of failure should be verified by calculation or by testing. For example, a guard rail forming part of an edge protection system will have enough structural strength to act as edge protection but it will be unlikely that it would have been designed to withstand the dynamic and static forces of fall arrest. Before it is used as an anchorage for a fall arrest lanyard and harness, its strength would need to be reassessed by a competent engineer.

16 When using horizontal anchor lines (sometimes referred to as running lines) as lifelines, it is important to limit the number of workers to that prescribed by the manufacturer, and to obtain performance calculations of end forces before use. This is because forces in horizontal anchor lines can be magnified many times at the anchor points in the event of a fall.

Inspecting equipment and anchors

17 All parts of a personal fall-protection system should be subject to an inspection regime that includes pre-use checks and periodic detailed examinations. It may also require additional interim inspections.

18 Keep equipment clean and dry, and properly stored. Wet equipment should be thoroughly dried before storage. Equipment should not be altered or repaired, unless this has been authorised by the manufacturer.

Pre-use checks

19 Before each use, equipment should be visually inspected and checked by hand, in accordance with the manufacturer's instructions, by a competent person (preferably the user). If any defects are found the equipment should not be used. The checks should include any tensioned safety lines.

Detailed examination of equipment

20 Periodic detailed examinations should be carried out by a competent person in accordance with the manufacturer's instructions. The examination should be recorded. The recommended minimum frequencies for such examinations are:

- because of its susceptibility to wear, damage and degradation, equipment made from webbing, rope or textiles should not be used unless it has been examined in detail at least once in the preceding six months. Detailed guidance on inspecting equipment made from webbing or rope is given in *Inspecting fall arrest equipment made from webbing or rope* INDG367;[24]
- other parts, including anchors/anchor systems, should not be used unless they have been examined in detail at least once in the preceding 12 months.

Interim inspections

21 Interim detailed examinations may be required in addition to pre-use checks and six- or 12-monthly detailed examinations. They will be required where the employer's risk assessment has identified a risk that could result in the system deteriorating significantly before the next planned inspection, eg exposure to grit blasting or paints or chemicals. The interim examination should be recorded.

Post-fall inspection

22 If a fall-protection system has had to arrest a fall, or has been subject to other high-shock loads, then none of the elements in that system should be used until they have either undergone a detailed examination or been replaced in accordance with the manufacturer's instructions.

Inspection of rescue equipment

23 The manufacturer may supply certain items of personal fall protection equipment used for rescue purposes in sealed transparent packaging. If the seal is not broken, these items do not require interim inspections. However, after a specified period (often three years), they must be returned to the manufacturer for inspection and resealing.

24 Additional guidance is given in:

- BS 8437:2005 *Code of practice for selection, use and maintenance of personal fall protection systems and equipment for use in the workplace;*[30] and
- *Inspecting fall arrest equipment made from webbing or rope* INDG367.

Work-restraint systems

25 Work-restraint systems are sometimes referred to, inaccurately, as fall restraint. In a work-restraint system, the position of the anchor point(s), when combined with the user's PPE, allows a worker to carry out their job but prevents them from reaching any position from which they could fall. This type of system increases user safety and reduces the need for rescue provision. **Where practicable a work-restraint system should be used in preference to fall arrest.**

26 A working area will often have more than one edge or other place from which a worker could fall. For example, a particular roof area may have edges along the eaves and along the gables; it may also contain fragile roof lights. Make sure that the work-restraint system prevents the user from reaching any location from which they could fall.

Fall-arrest systems

27 Fall-arrest systems should incorporate some form of energy absorber or an energy-dissipating element. This must make sure that, in the event of a fall, the forces on the user do not exceed 6 kN and will help reduce the transfer of forces to the structure to which the system is attached.

28 For a fall-arrest system to function correctly there must be adequate clearance beneath the work area, eg:

A system comprising a full body harness and a 2 m long lanyard with an energy absorber, anchored to a 20 m horizontal anchor line at foot level could require up to 7.75 m of clearance below the anchorage. This is made up as follows:

Original length of the lanyard plus shock absorber	**2.0 m**
Maximum allowable shock absorber extension	**1.75 m**
Deflection of the anchor line cable during the fall arrest	**1.5 m**
Allowance for displacement of the worker, stretch in the full body harness and the clearance below the user's feet after the arrest	**2.5 m**
Total	**7.75 m**

29 If a fall-arrest system is in use then the employer should consider and plan for rescuing or retrieving a fallen worker. There should always be a rescue plan in place, with the necessary equipment and trained people to carry out a rescue in safety without putting more workers at risk. A fallen worker should be rescued as quickly as possible (see paragraphs 46–51).

30 It is good practice to install fall-arrest system anchor points as high above the user as possible, as this reduces forces, risk of injury and, in the event of a fall, makes rescue easier. Anchors should not be installed below foot level.

31 If using retractable fall arresters (sometimes called 'inertia reels'), they should be anchored vertically above the user so that the extendable line between the reel and the user runs largely vertically. If you wish to use a retractable fall arrester in any other orientation you should get confirmation from the manufacturer that it has been tested and found safe for use in the desired orientation.

32 Where there is a risk that a worker will fall from a leading edge and the lanyard or extendable line from a retractable fall arrester will come into direct contact with the edge of the structure during the fall arrest, it is important that **only** equipment tested for this particular circumstance is used. You **must** seek confirmation from the manufacturer that the device is fit for the purpose you wish to use it for. Failure to follow this advice could lead to the catastrophic failure of the fall-protection system.

33 Several national and European standards apply to fall-protection systems and the individual elements such as lanyards, harnesses, anchors etc. The two British Standards listed below give general advice and list the other relevant standards:

- BS 7883:2005 *Code of Practice for the design, selection, installation, use and maintenance of anchor devices conforming to BS EN 795*;[31] and
- BS 8437:2005 *Code of practice for selection, use and maintenance of personal fall protection systems and equipment for use in the workplace.*

34 The Work at Height Safety Association website contains guidance notes on the use of fall protection equipment: www.wahsa.org.uk.

Appendix 4 Fragility: Tests and specifications

1 There is now a widely accepted standard of performance within the UK to define what a 'non-fragile profiled sheeted roof' is. The test to show non-fragility for a roofing assembly has been drawn up by the Advisory Committee for Roofsafety (ACR) and is published in *Test for non-fragility of roofing assemblies*.[16]

2 UK manufacturers of profiled roofing sheets are aware of the performance requirements of the ACR non-fragility tests and have designed their products for the industrial, commercial and agricultural roofing markets such that, when fully fixed to their fixing requirements, the roof assembly will be non-fragile. The advent of the ACR test has seen a dramatic improvement in the technical performance of all industrial profiled sheeting in the last ten years.

3 There are three categories to passing the ACR test:

- **Non-fragile Class C:** The roof assembly retains a dropped load after one drop but fails to retain the load on the second drop. This is the minimum standard now accepted for a non-fragile roof. In practice, this means that if someone slipped and fell on to a Class C roof, it is likely that they would damage the roof such that it would need repairs to maintain weather resistance and a non-fragile status.
- **Non-fragile Class B:** The roof assembly retains a dropped load after two drops. In practice, this means that a person could fall twice in the same area and the roof would still support their weight. However Class B means that damage will have been done to the roof that may impair long-term weather resistance and reduce the time that the non-fragile status is maintained.
- **Non-fragile Class A:** The roof assembly retains a dropped load after two drops and there are no signs of any damage to the roof assembly that will affect the roof's long-term weather resistance.

4 The ACR test is a demanding test with good safety factors built in. A Class C performance is fully acceptable as a standard of non-fragility. A Class B rating will normally be achieved with profiled metal assemblies and profiled roof lights. A Class A rating is unlikely to be achieved using normally accepted profiled materials. A Class A rating would typically be required where vehicle access was required on the roof.

5 Achieving a non-fragile roof, including all roof lights, at the construction phase is now commonplace and anything less should not be accepted.

6 However, as non-fragile roofs become more common, there is a serious risk that roof workers become complacent and do not recognise that a non-fragile roof will, at some point in time, become fragile. Fragility will eventually occur for one or many of the following reasons:

- the fixings were badly fixed leading to excessive wear around the fixing;
- the fixing washers have failed due to overtightening, leading to sheet and fixing corrosion;
- the protective surface of the profiled sheeting was damaged by foot traffic during construction or during the roof maintenance phase, which will lead to an early failure of the sheet's performance;
- any slip or fall on to the roof may damage the assembly, which could lead to early corrosion failure;
- external atmospheric conditions could lead to early failure of the sheet's performance, eg saline or factory process;
- the sheets and fixings have reached the end of their design life; and/or
- if a roof was built before 2000, it may well have been fragile when constructed.

7 Further information on how to work with fragile roofs can be found in *Safe working on fragile roofs*.[18]

Appendix 5 Demolition involving asbestos cement roof sheets

1 If a building contains any asbestos it should be removed **before** demolition in accordance with the Control of Asbestos Regulations 2012 and the Approved Code of Practice (ACOP) *Work with materials containing asbestos* L143.[32]

2 Some asbestos-containing materials may only be removed by licensed contractors once they have notified HSE. The person in control of the demolition job must make sure this has been done before starting any further removal or demolition works.

3 Demolition involving asbestos cement sheets is not licensed work (providing the 4 hour and 10 minute control limits are not exceeded) but it may be notifiable to HSE. For notifiable non-licensed work (NNLW), employers also have additional requirements to notify work with asbestos to the relevant enforcing authority, ensure medical examinations are carried out, and maintain registers of work (health records).

4 An employer needs to decide before starting work whether or not it is notifiable. To do this they will need to consider the task(s) to be undertaken and the nature and condition of the material. See the summary in paragraph 7 below and more detailed advice is given on HSE's website www.hse.gov.uk/asbestos/licensing/notifiable-non-licensed-work.htm. Normal weathering does not attract notification duties.

5 There are two general methods available to contractors intending to demolish structures of this type:

- by hand; or
- by remote methods.

6 To choose the most suitable method, demolition contractors have to weigh up the following factors:

- the exposure of worker(s) to asbestos fibres;
- contamination of the surrounding environment by asbestos dust and, in particular, exposing anyone downwind of the site to asbestos fibres;
- the risk of falling, especially through the asbestos cement roof; and
- how difficult the asbestos is to access.

7 Each job must be considered on its merits but, in general, individual removal of sheets intact by hand will not be notifiable; remote demolition by machine involving deliberate breakage of sheets and consequent potential release of and exposure to asbestos fibres will be notifiable as NNLW.

Risk of exposure and contamination

8 Asbestos cement is a grey, hard, brittle material normally containing 10–15% asbestos fibre. It is a dense material with a density greater than 1 tonne/m^3 and when soaked in water for at least 15 minutes will absorb less than 30% of its own weight of water as the asbestos fibres are tightly bound with cement.

9 To release the asbestos fibres from the asbestos cement, the material needs to be aggressively abraded. Activities such as sawing, drilling, wire brushing or crushing the material by tracking back and forth with heavy machinery are likely to produce dust containing asbestos fibres if the material is dry.

10 Any material containing more than 0.1% asbestos is classified as 'hazardous waste' and can only be carried on the road by a registered waste carrier consigning it to a licensed asbestos dump. Your local Environment Agency area office will be able to advise on disposal.

Risk of falling

11 Many asbestos cement products (such as roof sheets, slates, cladding, down pipes and gutters) are located at height and are fragile, and therefore present a risk of falls. Asbestos cement sheet is a fragile material in accordance with the *Test for non-fragility of roofing assemblies*[16] (see paragraphs 166–198).

Demolition

Method 1 – by hand

12 Due to the potential for high levels of dust containing asbestos fibres to be created during remote demolition, the extra dust created during the subsequent clean up and the risk to anyone downwind of the site, demolition by hand is the preferred option.

13 When working with asbestos-containing materials, an adequate and sufficient risk assessment must be written down. Workers must be correctly supervised, trained and understand and follow the method statement they will be

working to. They must have a thorough knowledge of the materials, equipment and tools they will be using, all in accordance with the ACOP *Work with materials containing asbestos* L143.

14 If the asbestos cement sheets are in reasonable condition and it is possible to provide safe access and a safe work surface (see paragraphs 166–198) then the sheets should be taken down whole – they should not be dropped or damaged. They are best disposed of by careful transfer to covered lorries or skips, or by wrapping intact in heavy-duty sheet plastic.

Method 2 – remote

15 In some circumstances remote demolition by machine (such as pusher arm or deliberate controlled collapse) is necessary (eg if the asbestos sheets are in poor condition, ie liable to break when handled, or safe access cannot be provided and the risk of falling is too great).

16 **Careful** remote demolition gives rise to low dust concentrations of about 0.1 f/ml, and so a risk assessment may indicate that the control level of 0.1 f/ml of air averaged over a four-hour period may be exceeded and a licensed asbestos contractor will be required. Before remote demolition is started serious consideration must be given to how anyone downwind of the demolition will be protected from what may be dust levels above 0.1 f/ml, and subsequent clearance activities may result in a much higher concentration of more than 1 f/ml.

17 To reduce the risk of the spread of contamination, contractors should take precautions including the following:

- carry out and complete the work before the rest of the structure is demolished;
- keep the material wet with gentle spraying;
- remove waste and debris from the site by hand as soon as possible to prevent it being disturbed, eg by moving vehicles. If material cannot be removed immediately, cover with heavy-duty polythene;
- take care to avoid plant being driven over asbestos cement sheet;
- broken asbestos cement sheet should be picked by hand where possible; if gathered by mechanical means, should be well wetted to minimise fibre release. It should not be bulldozed into a pile. Toothed buckets should not be used;
- fine debris or waste liable to generate dust should be placed in suitable closed containers. Larger pieces of asbestos cement are best disposed of by careful transfer to covered lorries or skips; and
- containers (bags, skips etc) used for asbestos waste must be correctly labelled and disposed of to a licensed waste tip.

Personal protective equipment (PPE)

18 Where dust concentrations are below the 0.1 f/ml averaged over four hours control limit then disposable masks suitable for working with asbestos should be worn (ie those rated at FFP3) and workers should be provided with disposable overalls which should be safely disposed of with the masks as hazardous waste at the end of every shift.

Training

19 People who carry out any work on asbestos materials must be trained and supervised properly. You need training even if you have worked with asbestos in the past. Training must include detailed information on:

- recognising asbestos;
- how asbestos can affect your health;
- the added dangers of smoking;
- the uses and likely locations for asbestos in buildings;
- what work you are allowed to do by law;
- what the law requires you to do;
- what methods to use;
- what equipment you need to do the job properly;
- how to choose, use and look after personal protective equipment;
- recognising and dealing with other dangers such as work at height;
- decontamination of yourself and work areas;
- emergency procedures; and
- waste disposal.

20 Refresher training is needed every year, or more often if:

- work methods change;
- the type of equipment used changes; or
- the type of work changes a lot.

21 Supervise the task – make sure workers follow the rules.

22 See *Work with materials containing asbestos. Control of Asbestos Regulations 2006. Approved Code of Practice and guidance* L143 for more specific information about training and work with asbestos.

Public concerns

23 To members of the public the remote method appears noisy, dusty and often uncontrolled. They are often concerned about this type of demolition when they know or suspect the building was roofed or clad with asbestos cement. To alleviate concerns, contractors are advised to:

- keep the neighbours informed about the work;
- consult the local environmental health department; and
- carry out regular dust readings downwind of the site.

Appendix 6 Safe operation of bitumen boilers

1 Bitumen boilers are widely used in work on flat roofs. Three types of risk need to be controlled when using these boilers:

- fire and explosion risk from storage and use of liquefied petroleum gas (LPG);
- risk of burning from contact with hot bitumen; and
- risk of respiratory irritation from excessive inhalation of bitumen fumes.

2 Providing the right equipment, keeping it in good condition and training workers in basic good practice will help to reduce accidents to workers and the public.

3 When setting up the boiler, a number of basic safety guidelines should be followed:

- Stand the boiler on a firm, level surface, which should be non-combustible and capable of carrying the load. Do not site the boiler inside a building or in any enclosed space.
- When based on the roof surface, set the boiler in a tray, with a greater capacity than the contents of the boiler, to contain any spillage. Set the tray on a fire-resistant material.
- Set up the gas cylinder at least 3 m away from the boiler during use, unless a suitable protective shield is fitted.
- All additional gas cylinders should be safely stored at least 6 m away.
- Make sure that hoses are of the correct type, in good condition and properly connected. A pressure regulator must be fitted to all gas cylinders.
- Use a thermostatically controlled boiler to provide maximum safety.
- Check for leaks before use: soapy water is ideal – **never** use a naked flame.
- Do not smoke or allow others to smoke.
- Have at least one fire extinguisher close by (9 litre foam or 9 kg dry powder). **Never** use water to combat a bitumen fire. Ideally, also keep two boxes of sand (or similar) to hand.
- A bucket of cold water should be kept near the workspace for use only in the case of bitumen burn.
- Never leave the boiler unattended when lit or hot.
- Protect the boiler with suitable barriers where other workers or the public may have access.
- Unless they are in a safe location, remove the gas cylinders when the boiler is not in use to prevent unauthorised use or interference.
- Keep other combustibles (such as paper, packaging etc) well away from the boiler cylinders.

4 While heating the bitumen:

- before lighting up, the burner should be removed from under the boiler (if this is possible), lit and then replaced. This avoids any possibility of a build-up of gas under the boiler during the lighting process. Generally, follow the maker's instructions on lighting up;
- do not exceed the recommended operating temperature for the particular grade of bitumen used;
- when heating from cold, keep heating rates low until the bitumen is clearly liquid and any water has been driven off;
- add bitumen carefully – avoid splashing; and
- gas-fired bitumen heating boilers should **never** be used for heating cut-back bitumens. These bitumens contain solvents which can be easily ignited by such open-flame heating – a rapidly escalating fire would ensue.

5 Precautions during use:

- keep water away from hot bitumen;
- never use a ladle to remove bitumen – use the draw-off tap;
- wear suitable eye protection, foot protection and gloves;
- wear suitable clothing to avoid skin contact with splashes;
- exposure to fumes should be minimised by working, as far as reasonably practicable, on the upwind side of the hot works, and if required, by wearing a simple face filter;
- do not heat the bitumen drums unless they are designed for that purpose;
- keep the lid on the boiler as much as possible. In the case of a boiler fire, close the lid immediately, then turn off the gas supply valve and move the gas cylinder away from the area;
- make sure that bitumen boilers do not boil over. If this does occur, the gas supply valve must be turned off and the cylinder moved away from any burning bitumen;
- regularly check the boiler temperature and level. Alternatively, use a boiler with thermostatic controls;
- carry bitumen in proper containers, eg lidded buckets;
- the area around the boiler itself, and the route from the boiler to where the bitumen is used, should be kept clear, safe and unhindered; and
- make sure that lifting equipment used, eg pulleys, blocks ropes etc is suitable and in good condition, before and after each job.

6 After use:

- turn off the gas firstly at the burner, then at the cylinders; and
- prevent build-up of bitumen on the outside of the boiler by regularly removing drips and splashes. Excessive spillages should be dealt with promptly.

7 At all times:

- make sure the boiler does not overheat or run low;
- turn the gas off before leaving the boiler unattended, even for a short time;
- never apply direct heat to pipes or valves, or to the outside of the boiler;
- turn off the burner and allow it to cool until the bitumen is solid before moving or towing the boiler on a lorry or trailer; and
- follow general advice on safe storage and use of LPG given in *Storage of full and empty LPG cylinders and cartridges*[33] and *Containers attached to mobile gas-fired equipment*.[34]

8 Workers and supervisors should be trained in specific first-aid procedures for bitumen burns. This should be supported by written instructions clearly available on site. A concise burns handling card can be downloaded from the safety page on the Refined Bitumen Association website: www.bitumenuk.com. Further information is given in industry codes of practice for the safe operation of propane-fired bitumen boilers.[35,36]

Appendix 7 Edge protection

1 When working on roofs, new or old, it is essential to protect workers from falling from the edge of the roof. 'Edge protection' is the term commonly used to describe measures that can be used to prevent workers falling from the roof edge.

2 There are a number of popularly used systems:

- full scaffold;
- scaffold handrail;
- proprietary guard rail systems; and
- netting systems.

3 The most appropriate system will depend on several factors:

- duration of work;
- type of roof;
- roof slope; and
- size and weight of materials being used.

4 The decision on which type of edge protection to use must be made by a competent person who has all of the information about the work that is to be undertaken. Similarly, the person who installs the edge protection must be competent in its installation and dismantling.

5 Where roofs are steep and/or materials are large or heavy the risk is greater and so a full scaffold may be the most appropriate. At the other end of the spectrum, if the work is to be carried out on a non-fragile flat roof then a simple handrail, or possibly a system using counterweights to support a handrail, will be adequate. Consider using a system that is also appropriate to the duration of the work – an access platform that requires minutes to position to carry out minor work may involve less risk of working at height than a comprehensive scaffolding solution which takes a large number of man hours to install and dismantle.

6 BS EN 13374[37] is the European Norm for edge protection design.

7 The Advisory Committee for Roofsafety has produced practical guidance on the use of various edge protection systems and their applications – see *Practical methods of providing edge protection for working on roofs*.[38]

References and further reading

References

1 *Health and safety in construction* HSG150 (Third edition) HSE Books 2006 ISBN 978 0 7176 6182 4 www.hse.gov.uk/pubns/books/hsg150.htm

2 *Managing health and safety in construction. Construction (Design and Management) Regulations 2007. Approved Code of Practice* L144 HSE Books 2007 ISBN 978 0 7176 6223 4 www.hse.gov.uk/pubns/books/l144.htm

3 *Tower scaffolds* Construction Information Sheet CIS10(rev4) HSE Books 2005 www.hse.gov.uk/pubns/conindex.htm

4 *The selection and management of mobile elevating work platforms* Construction Information Sheet CIS58 HSE Books 2008 www.hse.gov.uk/pubns/conindex.htm

5 *Safe use of ladders and stepladders: An employers' guide* Leaflet INDG402 HSE Books 2005 (priced packs ISBN 978 0 7176 6105 3) www.hse.gov.uk/falls/stepladders.htm

6 *A toolbox talk on leaning ladder and stepladder safety* Leaflet INDG403 HSE Books 2005 (priced packs ISBN 978 0 7176 6105 3) www.hse.gov.uk/construction/resources/toolboxtalks.htm

7 *Top tips for ladder and stepladder safety* Pocket card INDG405 HSE Books 2005 (priced packs ISBN 978 0 7176 6127 5) www.hse.gov.uk/falls/stepladders.htm

8 *Roofing and cladding in windy conditions* NFRC 2006 (available from NFRC Publications Ltd, Roofing House, 31 Worship Street, London EC2A 2DY)

9 BS 7375:2010 *Distribution of electricity on construction and demolition sites. Code of practice* British Standards Institution

10 *Health and safety guide for aerial and satellite businesses* April 2009 Confederation of Aerial Industries Limited

11 *Disposing of asbestos waste* NetRegs http://environment-agency.gov.uk/netregs/113180.aspx

12 *Trussed Rafter Association Technical Handbook* 1997 (available from Trussed Rafter Association, PO Box 571, Chesterfield S40 9DH)

13 *Slater's heel* Guidance Sheet E NFRC 2008 www.nfrc.co.uk

14 BS 5534:2003+A1:2010 *Code of practice for slating and tiling (including shingles)* British Standards Institution

15 *Graded battens for slating and tiling* Technical Bulletin 33 NFRC www.nfrc.co.uk

16 *Test for non-fragility of profile sheeted roofing assemblies* ACR(M)001:2011 (Fourth edition) ACR 2011 www.roofworkadvice.info

17 *Recommended practice for work on profiled sheeted roofs* ACR(CP)001:2007 (Revision 3) ACR 2007 www.roofworkadvice.info

18 *Safe working on fragile roofs or roofs with fragile elements* ACR(CP)002:2012 (Second edition) ACR 2012 www.roofworkadvice.info

19 *Protecting the public: Your next move* HSG151 HSE Books 2009 ISBN 978 0 7176 6294 4 www.hse.gov.uk/pubns/books/hsg151.htm

20 *Safety signs and signals. The Health and Safety (Safety Signs and Signals) Regulations 1996. Guidance on Regulations* L64 HSE Books 2009 ISBN 978 0 7176 6359 0 www.hse.gov.uk/pubns/books/l64.htm

21 *Recommended practice for the use of safety nets for roofwork* ACR(CP)003:2008 ACR 2008 www.roofworkadvice.info

22 *Best practice for the specification and installation of metal cladding and secondary steelwork* P346 Steel Construction Institute 2007

23 BS 8454:2006 *Code of practice for the delivery of training and education for work at height and rescue* British Standards Institution

24 *Inspecting fall arrest equipment made from webbing or rope* Leaflet INDG367 HSE Books 2002 (priced packs ISBN 978 0 7176 2552 9) www.hse.gov.uk/pubns/conindex.htm

25 *Workplace health, safety and welfare. Workplace (Health, Safety and Welfare) Regulations 1992. Approved Code of Practice* L24 (Twelfth edition) HSE Books 1992 ISBN 978 0 7176 0413 5 www.hse.gov.uk/pubns/books/l24.htm

26 BS EN 1263-1:2002 *Safety nets. Safety requirements, test methods* British Standards Institution

27 BS EN 1263-2:2002 *Safety nets. Safety requirements for the positioning limits* British Standards Institution

28 BS 8411:2007 *Code of practice for safety nets on construction sites and other works* British Standards Institution

29 *International Code of Practice (ICOP)* Industrial Rope Access Trade Association 2012

30 BS 8437:2005 *Code of practice for selection, use and maintenance of personal fall protection systems and equipment for use in the workplace* British Standards Institution

31 BS 7883:2005 *Code of practice for the design, selection, installation, use and maintenance of anchor devices conforming to BS EN 795* British Standards Institution

32 *Work with materials containing asbestos. Control of Asbestos Regulations 2006. Approved Code of Practice and guidance* L143 HSE Books 2006 ISBN 978 0 7176 6206 7 www.hse.gov.uk/pubns/books/l143.htm

33 *Storage of full and empty LPG cylinders and cartridges* Code of Practice 7 LP Gas Association 2004 www.uklpg.org/index.php

34 *Containers attached to mobile gas-fired equipment* Code of Practice 10 LP Gas Association 2005

35 *Model Code of Safe Practice Part 11: Bitumen safety code (Fourth edition, revised)* Energy Institute 2005 ISBN 978 0 8529 3402 9 (Fourth edition, revised) Energy Institute 2005 ISBN 978 0 85293 402 9

36 *Use of heat for roofing operations* Guidance sheet F NFRC www.nfrc.co.uk

37 BS EN 13374:2004 *Temporary edge protection systems. Product specification, test methods* British Standards Institution

38 *Practical methods of providing edge protection for working on roofs* ACR(CP)006:2009 ACR 2009 www.roofworkadvice.info

Further reading

Management of health and safety at work. Management of Health and Safety at Work Regulations 1999. Approved Code of Practice and guidance L21 (Second edition) HSE Books 2000 ISBN 978 0 7176 2488 1 www.hse.gov.uk/pubns/books/l21.htm

Five steps to risk assessment Leaflet INDG163(rev3) HSE Books 2011 (priced packs ISBN 978 0 7176 6440 5) www.hse.gov.uk/pubns/raindex.htm

CDM 2007 – Construction work sector guidance for designers C662 CIRIA 2007 ISBN 978 0 86017 662 6 (available from www.ciriabooks.com)

Successful health and safety management HSG65 (Second edition) HSE Books 1997 ISBN 978 0 7176 1276 5 www.hse.gov.uk/pubns/books/hsg65.htm

Managing asbestos in buildings Leaflet INDG223(rev5) HSE Books 2012 (priced packs ISBN 978 0 7176 6487 0) www.hse.gov.uk/pubns/indg223.htm

Information on first-aid arrangements required in the workplace: www.hse.gov.uk/firstaid/index.htm

Lifting equipment at work: A brief guide to the law Leaflet INDG290 HSE Books 1999 (priced pack ISBN 978 0 7176 2430 0) www.hse.gov.uk/pubns/liftindex.htm

Further information

For information about health and safety, or to report inconsistencies or inaccuracies in this guidance, visit www.hse.gov.uk/. You can view HSE guidance online and order priced publications from the website. HSE priced publications are also available from bookshops.

British Standards can be obtained in PDF or hard copy formats from BSI: http://shop.bsigroup.com or by contacting BSI Customer Services for hard copies only
Tel: 020 8996 9001 email: cservices@bsigroup.com.

Printed and published by the Health and Safety Executive 09/12